ROUGH GUIDES

T0022138

POCKET **ROUGH GUIDE**

PRAGUE

written and researched by
MARC DI DUCA
this edition updated by
BETH WILLIAMS

CONTENTS

PRAGUE

With some six hundred years of architecture virtually untouched by natural disaster or war, few other European capitals look quite as beautiful as Prague. Straddling the winding River Vltava, with a steep wooded hill to one side, the city retains much of its medieval layout, and its rich mantle of Baroque, Rococo and Art Nouveau buildings has successfully escaped the vanities and excesses of modern redevelopment.

The *Head of Franz Kafka* sculpture by Czech artist David Černý

Art Nouveau building in the Old Town Square

Physically, Prague may have weathered the twentieth century very well but it suffered in other ways. The city that produced the music of Dvořák and Smetana, the literature of Čapek and Kafka, and modernist architecture to rival Bauhaus, was forced to endure a brutal Nazi occupation. Prague had always been a multiethnic city, with a large Jewish and German-speaking population – in the aftermath of the war, only the Czechs were left. Then for forty years, during the Communist period, the city lay hidden behind the Iron Curtain, seldom visited by Westerners. All that changed in the 1990s, and nowadays Prague is one of the most popular European city-break destinations, with a highly developed tourist industry and a large expat population who, if nothing else, help to boost the city's nightlife.

Prague is divided into two unequal halves by the river, which meanders through the heart of the capital and provides the city with one of its most enduring landmarks: Charles Bridge. Built during the city's medieval golden

When to visit

Prague is very popular, which means that the streets around the main sights are jam-packed with tourists for much of the year. If you can, it's best to avoid the summer months, when temperatures sometimes soar above 30ºC, and you have to fight your way across Charles Bridge. The best times to visit, in terms of weather, are May and September. The winter months can be very chilly in Prague, but if you don't mind the cold, the city does look good in the snow and the crowds are manageable. Christmas and New Year are perfect as there are Christmas markets right across town, and plenty of mulled wine and hot punch to keep you warm.

age, this stone bridge, with its parade of Baroque statuary, still forms the chief link between the more central old town, or Staré Město, on the right bank, and Prague's hilltop castle on the left. The castle is a vast complex, which towers over the rest of the city and supplies the classic picture-postcard image of Prague. Spread across the slopes beneath the castle are the wonderful cobbled streets and secret walled gardens of Malá Strana, little changed in the two hundred years since Mozart walked them.

With a population of just one and a quarter million, Prague (Praha to the Czechs) is relatively small as capital cities go. It originally developed as four separate self-governing towns and a Jewish ghetto, whose individual identities and medieval street plans have been preserved, to a greater or lesser extent, to this day. Almost everything of any historical interest lies within these compact central districts, and despite the twisting matrix of streets, it's easy enough to find your way around between the major landmarks. If you do use public transport, you'll find an extensive and picturesque tram network and a futuristic Soviet-built metro system that rivals most German cities. Price rises over the past decade mean Prague is no longer the budget destination it once was. However, one thing you can be sure of is that the beer is better and cheaper than anywhere else in the EU.

What's new

It's not so much what's new, but what's reopening soon in Prague that's big news. The National Museum (see page 81) spent several years beneath scaffolding before its grand doors swung open again in 2020, and the same is true of the Museum of Decorative Arts (see page 76), which has undergone a complete makeover. Vegetarian and vegan food has gained in popularity and there is an ever-growing crop of places specializing in meat-free versions of Czech classics, such as *Vegan's Prague* (see page 52) and *Maitrea* (see page 69). Prague is adding tram lines at a frantic pace and construction of blue metro line D from Náměstí Míru is underway and due to complete in 2023.

Where to...

Shop

Pařížská, in **Josefov**, is home to the city's swankiest stores, among them branches of the international fashion houses. Celetná in **Staré Město**, and Na příkopě on the border of **Nové Město**, also specialize in luxury goods. The city's most modern department store is My národní on **Národní**. Czechs have had their own malls – known as *pasáže* – since the 1920s, and new ones continue to sprout up. The mother of all malls is Palladium, on **Náměstí Republiky**, housed in a castellated former army barracks. For more offbeat, independent shops you need to explore the cobbled side streets of Staré Město and Nové Město.
OUR FAVOURITES: Truhlář marionety, see page 50. Art Deco, see page 66. Bric a Brac, see page 66.

Eat

As in many cities, the main thoroughfares in Prague aren't the best places to find somewhere to eat and drink. One or two grand Habsburg-era cafés survive on the main junctions of the city centre, but for the most part, the best cafés and restaurants are hidden away in the backstreets. There's an acute dearth of decent places in and around Prague Castle and Hradčany, while expensive restaurants predominate in **Malá Strana**. For a much wider choice of cafés, and of cuisine, head to **Staré Město** and the streets of **Nové Město** just south of Národní.
OUR FAVOURITES: Maitrea, see page 69. Naše maso, see page 69. Café Slavia, see page 98.

Drink

Given that the Czechs top the world league table of beer consumption, it comes as little surprise to find that Prague is a drinker's paradise. Wherever you are in the city, you're never far from a pub or bar. **Staré Město** has the highest concentration of drinking dens, but if you're looking for one of the city's new microbreweries or a traditional Czech pub (**pivnice**), you'll need to explore the residential streets of **Nové Město, Vinohrady** or **Holešovice**. Look out, too, for the many alfresco hangouts beside the river, on the islands, or in one of the public parks.
OUR FAVOURITES: U Černého vola, see page 39. Prague Beer Museum, see page 70. U zlatého tygra, see page 71.

Go out

Prague's often excellent theatre and concert venues are all very centrally located in **Staré Město** and **Nové Město**; the same is true for most small and medium-scale jazz and rock venues. **Žižkov** has more late-night pubs and bars than anywhere else, plus a smattering of gay and lesbian venues. One area that's has an emerging nightlife scene is **Holešovice**, in particular the old industrial and market area to the east of the metro line – the warehouse spaces here already shelter several of the city's newest clubs and venues. **Wenceslas Square** remains the traditional centre of Prague's seedier side.
OUR FAVOURITES: AghaRTA Jazz Centrum, see page 71. Storm Club, see page 111. Lucerna Music Bar, see page 89.

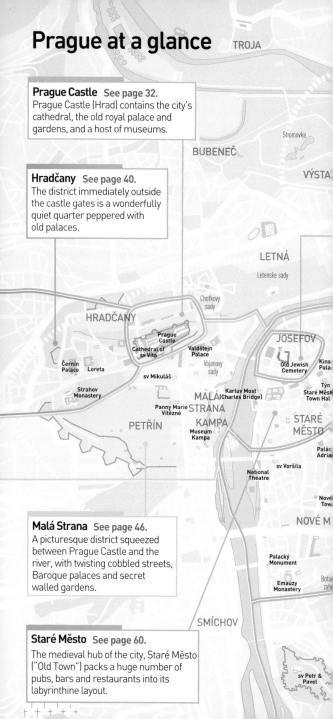

Prague at a glance

TROJA

Prague Castle See page 32.
Prague Castle (Hrad) contains the city's
cathedral, the old royal palace and
gardens, and a host of museums.

Stromovka

BUBENEČ

VÝSTA

Hradčany See page 40.
The district immediately outside
the castle gates is a wonderfully
quiet quarter peppered with
old palaces.

LETNÁ

Letenske sady

Chotkovy
sady

HRADČANY

Prague
Castle

JOSEFOV

Cathedral of
sv Víta

Valdštejn
Palace

Old Jewish
Cemetery

Kins
Pala

Vojanovy
sady

Černín
Palace

Loreta

Týn

sv Mikuláš

Staré Měst
Town Hal

Strahov
Monastery

Karluv Most
(Charles Bridge)

MALÁ

Panny Marie
Vítězné

STRANA

STARÉ
MĚSTO

KAMPA

PETŘÍN

Museum
Kampa

Palác
Adria

sv Voršila

National
Theatre

Nove
Tow

Malá Strana See page 46.
A picturesque district squeezed
between Prague Castle and the
river, with twisting cobbled streets,
Baroque palaces and secret
walled gardens.

NOVÉ M

Palacký
Monument

Emauzy
Monastery

Bota
zah

SMÍCHOV

Staré Město See page 60.
The medieval hub of the city, Staré Město
("Old Town") packs a huge number of
pubs, bars and restaurants into its
labyrinthine layout.

sv Petr &
Pavel

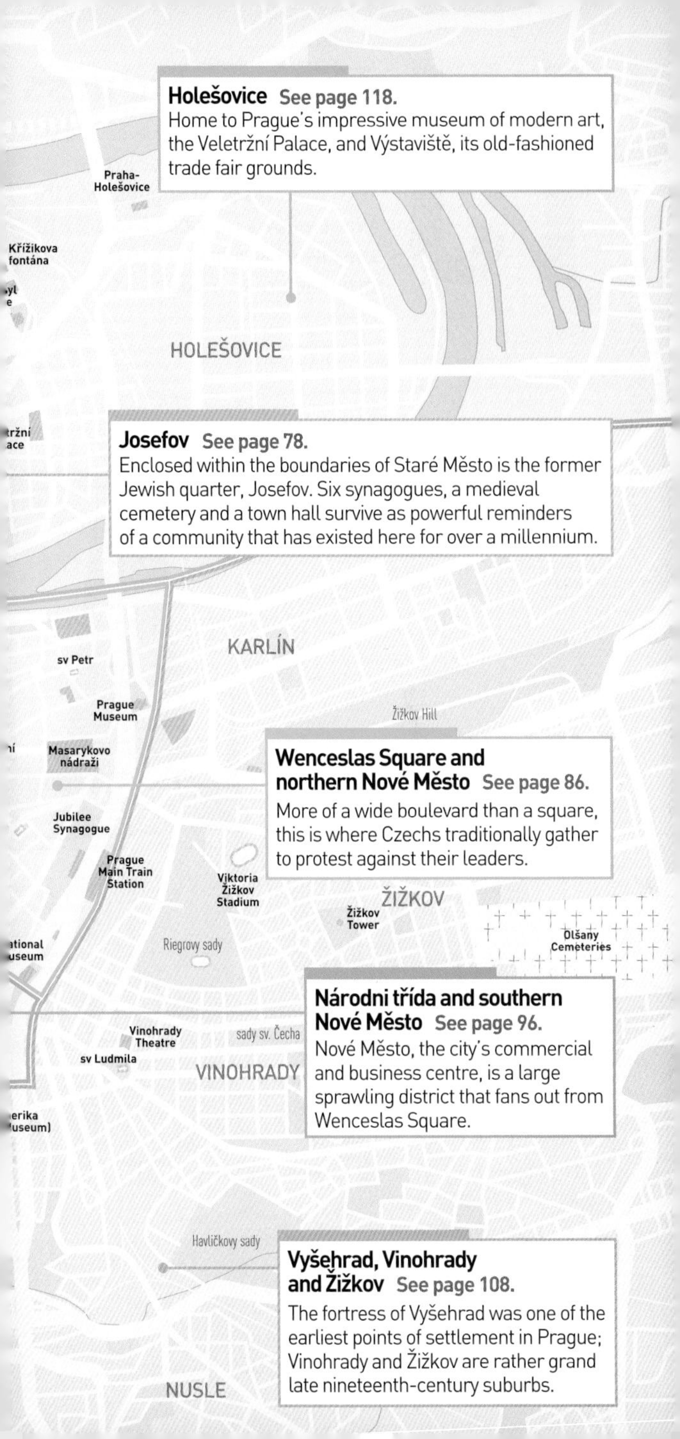

Holešovice See page 118.

Home to Prague's impressive museum of modern art, the Veletržní Palace, and Výstaviště, its old-fashioned trade fair grounds.

Josefov See page 78.

Enclosed within the boundaries of Staré Město is the former Jewish quarter, Josefov. Six synagogues, a medieval cemetery and a town hall survive as powerful reminders of a community that has existed here for over a millennium.

Wenceslas Square and northern Nové Město See page 86.

More of a wide boulevard than a square, this is where Czechs traditionally gather to protest against their leaders.

Národni třída and southern Nové Město See page 96.

Nové Město, the city's commercial and business centre, is a large sprawling district that fans out from Wenceslas Square.

Vyšehrad, Vinohrady and Žižkov See page 108.

The fortress of Vyšehrad was one of the earliest points of settlement in Prague; Vinohrady and Žižkov are rather grand late nineteenth-century suburbs.

Praha-Holešovice

Křižíkova fontána

HOLEŠOVICE

KARLÍN

sv Petr

Prague Museum

Žižkov Hill

Masarykovo nádraží

Jubilee Synagogue

Prague Main Train Station

Viktoria Žižkov Stadium

ŽIŽKOV

Žižkov Tower

Olšany Cemeteries

Riegrovy sady

Vinohrady Theatre

sady sv. Čecha

sv Ludmila

VINOHRADY

Havlíčkovy sady

NUSLE

15

Things not to miss

It's not possible to see everything that Prague has to offer in one trip – and we don't suggest you try. What follows is a selective taste of the city's highlights, from Baroque architecture to modern art.

> **Old Town Square**
See page 60
The city's showpiece square, lined with exquisite Baroque facades and overlooked by the town hall's famous astronomical clock.

< **Charles Bridge**
See page 54
Decorated with extravagant ecclesiastical statues, this medieval stone bridge is the city's most enduring monument.

∨ **Stavovské divadlo**
See page 64
The city's chief opera house has a glittering interior and a wealth of Mozart associations.

⟨ Vyšehrad
See page 104
This old Habsburg military fortress is now a great escape from the busy city.

⌄ Prague Castle
See page 26
Towering over the city, the castle is the ultimate picture-postcard image of Prague.

< **Convent of St Agnes**
See page 63
Gothic convent that provides the perfect setting for the National Collection of Medieval Art.

∨ **Strahov Monastery**
See page 38
Strahov boasts two monastic libraries adorned with fantastically ornate bookshelves and colourful frescoes.

THINGS NOT TO MISS

∧ UPM
See page 76
A treasure trove of Czech applied art, ranging from Meissen porcelain and Art Nouveau vases to avant-garde photography.

‹ Veletržní palac
See page 115
The city's premier modern art museum is housed in the functionalist Trade Fair Palace.

∧ **Obecní dům**
See page 84
Built in 1911 with the help of
leading Czech artists, this is the
city's finest Art Nouveau edifice.

∨ **Church of sv Mikuláš**
See page 41
Prague's finest Baroque church,
whose dome and tower dominate
the skyline of Malá Strana.

∧ Terraced Palace Gardens
See page 45
Pretty little Baroque gardens laid out on the terraced slopes beneath the castle.

< Café Louvre
See page 98
First-floor coffeehouse that roughly reproduces its illustrious 1902 predecessor.

< **Josefov**
See page 72
The former Jewish ghetto contains no fewer than six synagogues, a town hall and a remarkable medieval cemetery.

∨ **Wenceslas Square**
See page 80
The modern core of Prague, this sloping boulevard has been the scene of countless protests over the centuries.

THINGS NOT TO MISS

Day one in Prague

Prague Castle. See page 26. From Hradčanské náměstí, the square outside the main castle gates, you get an incredible view over Prague.

Cathedral of sv Víta. See page 26. Occupying centre stage in the castle's vast precincts is the city's Gothic cathedral.

Old Royal Palace. See page 27. Visit the palace's vast, rib-vaulted Vladislav Hall.

Story of Prague Castle. See page 29. Get the lowdown on past goings-on at Prague's most famous attraction – and learn a lot about Czech history in the process – at this modern exhibition.

The imposing facade of Prague Castle

Golden Lane. See page 31. Built in the sixteenth century for the imperial guards, this string of tiny little cottages pressed hard against the fortifications is now one of the most popular sights in the castle.

Lunch. See page 33. *Villa Richter*, situated in the middle of the castle vineyards, has superb views across the rooftops and river to Staré Město.

Church of sv Mikuláš. See page 41. This prominent Malá Strana landmark, tucked beneath the castle, is Prague's most ornate Baroque church.

Golden Lane

Charles Bridge. See page 54. Prague's famous medieval stone bridge is packed with people and lined with Baroque statues.

Museum Kampa. See page 46. This art gallery houses a permanent collection of two Czech artists: Kupka, a pioneer in abstract art, and the cubist sculptor Gutfreund.

Dinner. See page 51. Head to the pink house – otherwise known as *Kampa Park* – for romantic fine dining with serene riverside views.

Sculpture outside Museum Kampa

Day two in Prague

Obecní dům. See page 84. Book yourself on the morning tour round this cultural centre, an Art Nouveau jewel built in 1911.

Church of sv Jakub. See page 63. Enjoy one of Prague's finest ecclesiastical interiors at this Old Town church, with Prague's second-longest nave and a gruesome tale of theft and punishment.

Týn Church. See page 63. This giant Gothic church with twin, asymmetrical towers presides over Old Town Square.

Old Town Square. See page 60. Prague's spectacular square boasts a parade of Baroque facades, a giant statue of Jan Hus and an interactive astronomical clock.

Apple Museum. See page 58. One of the world's best computer technology museums is hidden in the backstreets between the Old Town Square and Charles Bridge.

Astronomical clock at Old Town Square

Lunch. See page 68. A classic Czech canteen, *Havelská koruna* is the place to go for plates of cheap and traditional comfort food.

Pinkas Synagogue. See page 75. Pay your respects to the 77,297 Czech Jews killed in the Holocaust, whose names cover the walls of this sixteenth-century synagogue.

Old Jewish Cemetery. See page 75. An evocative medieval cemetery in which the crowded gravestones mirror the cramped conditions in the ghetto.

Old-New Synagogue. See page 73. This thirteenth-century synagogue is the oldest active synagogue in Europe and one of Prague's earliest Gothic buildings.

Steve Jobs poster at the Apple Museum

Dinner. See page 69. Set in an underground cave-like restaurant, *Gruzie* is a great spot for traditional Georgian fare.

Pinkas Synagogue, Prague's second-oldest

Communist Prague

Despite forty-odd years of Communism, the regime left few traces on the city. However, several understated – and a couple ironic – memorials pay homage to the period.

Kinský Palace. See page 61. It was from the balcony of this Baroque palace that Klement Gottwald proclaimed the 1948 Communist takeover.

Museum of Communism. See page 83. It took an American expat to group together and exhibit the city's only collection of Communist memorabilia.

Jan Palach and Jan Zajíc Memorial. See page 80. In 1969, two young men took their own lives in protest against the Soviet invasion of the previous year. A simple plaque memorializes them.

Národní. See page 92. A simple bronze memorial commemorates the demonstration of November 17, 1989, which sparked the Velvet Revolution. An annual gathering takes place here on that date.

Memorial to the Victims of Communism. See page 48. Olbram Zoubek's striking memorial at the foot of Petřín hill pays tribute to those who were imprisoned, executed and went into exile.

Míčovna. See page 32. Seek out the hammer and sickle added to this fine Renaissance building in the Royal Gardens by the Communist restorers.

Metronome, Letná. See page 114. Take in the view from the metronome, which stands in the place where the world's largest Stalin statue once stood.

Žižkov Hill. See page 108. Once used as a Communist mausoleum, the Žižkov monument still boasts lashings of Socialist Realist decor.

Olšany cemeteries. See page 107. Pay your respects to the Red Army soldiers who lost their lives liberating the city in May 1945.

Statue of Lenin, Museum of Communism

Memorial to the Victims of Communism

Metronome at Letná

Kids' Prague

Most children will love Prague, with its rickety trams, street performers and buskers. Prague Castle, with its fairytale ramparts and towers, rarely disappoints either.

Funicular. See page 49. The funicular at Újezd, which takes you effortlessly to the top of Petřín hill, is part of the city's public transport and a fun way to sightsee.

Museum of Miniatures. See page 38. Kids will love this unusual museum with its tiny creations. Have fun looking through the magnifying glasses at Anatoly Konenko's miniscule masterpieces.

Petřín. See page 49. The Mirror Maze is a guaranteed hit with kids of all ages, and if you need to wear them out even more, encourage them to walk up the mini-Eiffel Tower for top views.

The funicular trundles to Petřín's peak

Changing of the Guard. See page 27. Prague Castle's armed guards are dressed like toy soldiers, and at noon every day they put on a bit of a show.

Tram #22. See page 132. This tram trundles from Prague Castle, round a hairpin bend and across the river to Karlovo náměstí.

Boat trip. See page 132. From April to September, you can take a 45-minute boat ride from PPS terminal near Palackého all the way to Troja, home of the zoo.

The Mirror Maze at Petřín

Prague Zoo. See page 118. A lot of money has gone into the zoo, and it shows: new enclosures, sensitive landscaping, and everything from elephants to zebras.

Truhlář marionety. See page 50. Prague is awash with puppets, but some of the best and most authentic are available at this small Malá Strana shop.

Výtopna Railway Restaurant. See page 89. Hearty, child-friendly food is delivered by train to your table. A fun concept that'll keep the kids entertained and well fed.

Changing of the Guard at Prague Castle

Green Prague

The Czech capital packs a lot of green spaces within its slender boundaries, many with medieval roots. Today, they provide a tranquil respite away from the tourist crush.

Terraced Palace Gardens. See page 45. The pretty terraced gardens beneath Prague Castle offer sweeping views of the city.

Stromovka. See page 117. This large leafy park stretches luxuriously between the Výstaviště and the chateau of Troja.

Royal Gardens. See page 32. Prague Castle's perfectly manicured gardens are famous for their disciplined crops of tulips.

Petřín. See page 49. This wooded hill on Prague's left bank provides a spectacular viewpoint over the city and has several popular attractions.

Slovanský ostrov. See page 95. The three leafy islands in the middle of the River Vltava are great places to picnic as you watch the resident swans. The most easily accessible is the Slovanský ostrov, with its grand Habsburg-era core.

Kampa. See page 46. The southern tip of Kampa island is a large park, a perfect central location for picnicking fun and sunbathing.

Botanic Gardens. See page 118. The highlight is the Fata Morgana glasshouse with its tropical plants and butterflies.

Vyšehrad. See page 104. This towering Habsburg fortress south of the centre is a superb place to escape the busy city.

Valdštejnská zahrada. See page 44. The formal Renaissance gardens unfurling from the Valdštejn Palace are populated by free-roaming peacocks.

Žižkov Hill. See page 108. This huge sprawl of parkland a short walk from the city centre is the ideal spot to flee the crowds.

The formal lines of the Royal Gardens

The fine views from Petřín

The picturesque waterways of Kampa

Ornate Prague

If there are two artistic and architectural styles that define the city, it's Baroque and turn-of-the-century Art Nouveau, best seen in Malá Strana and the New Town, respectively.

Loreto church. See page 37. A sumptuous Baroque pilgrimage complex with frescoed cloisters, a Black Madonna, and a stunning curation of gleaming reliquaries and monstrances.

Church of sv Mikuláš. See page 41. The city's most impressive Baroque church, crowned by a distinctive green dome and tower.

Strahov Monastery. See page 38. Strahov boasts two monastic libraries fitted with fantastically ornate bookshelves and splashed with colourful frescoes.

Baroque beauty: Loreto church

Charles Bridge statues. See page 54. It's the (mostly) Baroque statues that make this medieval bridge so unforgettable – the originals are scattered around various museums.

Prague Main Train Station. See page 81. Forget the modern, underground section, and head straight for the newly renovated 1909 Art Nouveau station, designed by Josef Fanta.

Mucha Museum. See page 83. Dedicated to Alfons Mucha, the Czech artist best known for his Art Nouveau Parisian posters.

Obecní dům. See page 84. One of Europe's finest Art Nouveau edifices, decorated by the leading Czech artists of the day.

Mucha's Window – St Vitus' Cathedral. See page 26. Alfons Mucha's Art Nouveau stained-glass window in St Vitus Cathedral dates from the mid-1920s.

Klementinum. See page 58. This huge Baroque complex, with its libraries, chapels and famous Astronomical Tower, is best explored on a tour.

The fine statues lining Charles Bridge

Prague's train station is a work of art

PLACES

Prague Castle poking above the skyline

Prague Castle

Prague's skyline is dominated by the vast hilltop complex of Prague Castle (Pražský hrad), which gazes out over the city centre from the west bank of the River Vltava. There's been a royal seat here for over a millennium, and it continues to serve as headquarters of the Czech president, but the castle is also home to several of Prague's chief tourist attractions: the Gothic Cathedral of sv Víta, the late medieval Old Royal Palace, the diminutive and picturesque Golden Lane and numerous museums and galleries. The best thing about the place, though, is that the public are free to roam around the atmospheric courtyards and take in the views from the ramparts from early in the morning until late at night.

Cathedral of sv Víta

MAP PAGE 28, POCKET MAP C11
Third courtyard. Charge.

Begun by Emperor Charles IV (1346–78), the **Cathedral** has a long and chequered history and wasn't finally completed until 1929. Once inside, it's difficult not to be impressed by the sheer height of the nave, and struck by the modern fixtures and fittings, especially the **stained-glass windows**, among them Alfons Mucha's superb *Cyril and Methodius* window, in the third chapel in the north wall, and František Bílek's wooden altar, in the north aisle.

Of the cathedral's numerous side chapels, the grand **Chapel of sv Václav** (better known as Wenceslas, of "Good King" fame), by the south door, is easily the

Cathedral of sv Víta

Visiting the castle

The castle precincts are open daily (🔵hrad.cz; charge). There are two main types of **multi-entry ticket** available for the sights within the castle. The **basic circuit ticket** covers the Cathedral of sv Víta, the Old Royal Palace, the Basilica of sv Jiří and Golden Lane. You can also purchase a separate ticket which includes the tower of the cathedral and a viewing gallery. Castle tickets are valid for two days and are available from various ticket offices. Temporary exhibitions, such as those held in the Imperial Stables and Riding School, all have separate admission charges.

Most people **approach the castle** from Malostranská metro station by taking the steep shortcut up the Staré zámecké schody, which brings you into the castle from the rear entrance to the east. A better approach is down Valdštejnská, and then up the more stately Zámecké schody, where you can stop and admire the view, or up the cobbled street of Nerudova, before entering the castle via the main gates. From April to October, you might also consider coming up through Malá Strana's wonderful terraced gardens (see page 45), which are connected to the castle gardens. Alternatively, you can take tram #22 from Malostranská metro, which deposits you at the Pražský hrad stop outside the Royal Gardens to the north of the castle.

The hourly **Changing of the Guard** at the main gates is a fairly subdued affair, but every day at noon there's a much more elaborate parade, accompanied by a modern fanfare. There are a couple of cafés within Prague Castle, though you'd be better off finding somewhere outside the castle precincts.

main attraction. The country's patron saint was killed by his pagan brother, Boleslav the Cruel, who later repented, converted, and apparently transferred his brother's remains to this very spot. The chapel's gilded walls are inlaid with over a thousand semi-precious stones, set around ethereal fourteenth-century frescoes of the Passion; meanwhile, the tragedy of Wenceslas unfolds dramatically above the cornice in sixteenth-century paintings.

The highlight of the ambulatory is the **Tomb of St John of Nepomuk**, a work of Baroque excess, sculpted in solid silver with free-flying angels holding up the heavy drapery of the baldachin. On the lid of the tomb, back-to-back with John himself, a cherub points to the martyr's severed tongue. Before you leave, check out the Habsburgs' sixteenth-century marble **Imperial Mausoleum**, in the centre of the choir, surrounded by a fine Renaissance grille. Below lies the claustrophobic **Royal Crypt**, the final resting place of emperors Charles IV and Rudolf II, plus various other Czech kings and queens.

You can also climb the cathedral's **Great Tower** (charge), from the south aisle. Outside the cathedral, don't forget to clock the **Golden Gate**, above the south door, decorated with a remarkable fourteenth-century mosaic of the Last Judgement.

Old Royal Palace (Starý královský palác)

MAP PAGE 28, POCKET MAP C11
Third courtyard. Charge.

The **Old Royal Palace** is a sandwich of royal apartments,

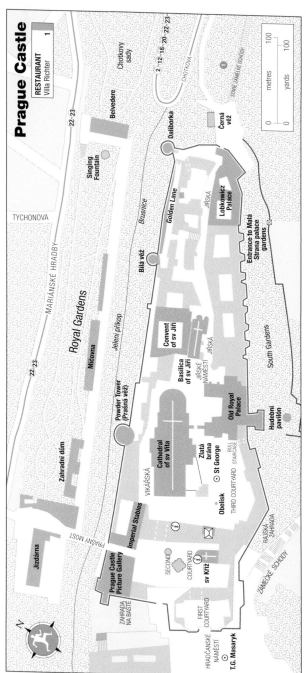

Prague Castle

RESTAURANT	
Villa Richter	1

The Powder Tower houses a Castle Guard exhibition

built one on top of the other by successive princes and kings of Bohemia, but left largely unused for the past three hundred years. It was in the **Vladislav Hall**, with its remarkable rib-vaulting which forms floral patterns on the ceiling, that the early Bohemian kings were elected, and that every president since 1918 has been sworn into office. From a staircase in the southwest corner, you can climb up to the Bohemian Chancellery, scene of Prague's **second defenestration**, when two Catholic governors, appointed by Ferdinand I, were thrown out of the window by a group of Protestant Bohemian noblemen in 1618. A canter down the Riders' Staircase will take you to the Gothic and Romanesque palace chambers containing "**The Story of Prague Castle**", an interesting, if long, exhibition on the development of the castle through the centuries.

Powder Tower (Prašná věž)

MAP PAGE 28, POCKET MAP C10
Vikářská. Charge.
The **Powder Tower** is where Rudolf II's team of alchemists were put to work trying to discover the secret of the philosopher's stone. The building now houses a small exhibition tracing the history of the Castle Guard.

Basilica of sv Jiří

MAP PAGE 28, POCKET MAP C10–C11
Jiřské náměstí.
Don't be fooled by the basilica's russet-red Baroque facade; inside is Prague's most beautiful Romanesque building, meticulously scrubbed clean and restored to re-create something like the honey-coloured stone basilica that replaced the original tenth-century church in 1173. The double staircase leading to the chancel is a remarkably harmonious late Baroque addition and now provides an atmospheric stage for chamber music concerts.

The choir vault contains a rare early thirteenth-century painting of the *New Jerusalem from Revelation*, while just to the right of the chancel is a series of sixteenth-century frescoes of the burial chapel of sv Ludmila, Bohemia's first Christian martyr and grandmother of St Wenceslas.

Golden Lane is lined with dinky cottages

Convent of sv Jiří (Jiřský klášter)

MAP PAGE 28, POCKET MAP C10
Jiřské náměstí.

Bohemia's earliest monastery was founded in 973 by Prince Boleslav II and his sister Mlada, who was its first mother superior. A fire in 1142 resulted in the addition of the main apse and two steeples which are still in place today, while the Early Baroque period saw it given its

Good King Wenceslas

Disappointingly, there's very little substance to the story related in the nineteenth-century English Christmas carol, "Good King Wenceslas looked out". For a start, **Václav** (**Wenceslas**) was only a duke and never a king (though he did become a saint); he wasn't even that "good", except in comparison with the rest of his family; Prague's St Agnes fountain, by which "yonder peasant dwelt", wasn't built until the thirteenth century; and he was killed a good three months before the Feast of Stephen (Boxing Day) – the traditional day for giving to the poor, hence the underlying narrative of the carol.

Born in 907, Václav inherited his title aged 13. His Christian grandmother, Ludmila, was appointed regent in preference to Drahomíra, his pagan mother, who subsequently had Ludmila murdered in 921. On coming of age in 925, Václav became duke in his own right and took a vow of celibacy, intent on promoting Christianity throughout the dukedom. Even so, the local Christians didn't take to him, and when he began making conciliatory overtures to the neighbouring Germans, they persuaded his pagan younger brother, Boleslav the Cruel, to do away with him. On September 20, 929, Václav was stabbed to death by Boleslav at the entrance to a church just outside Prague.

striking facade. In the eighteenth century, invading troops devastated the building, with later architects seeking to revive its original Romanesque style. Until 2012, the convent held an art collection from the National Gallery, but at the time of writing there were no plans to reopen it.

Golden Lane (Zlatá ulička)

MAP PAGE 28, POCKET MAP D10

A seemingly blind alley of brightly coloured miniature cottages, **Golden Lane** is by far the most popular sight in the castle, and during the day the whole street is crammed with sightseers. Originally built in the sixteenth century for the 24 members of Rudolf II's castle guard, the lane takes its name from the goldsmiths who followed a century later. By the nineteenth century, the whole street had become a kind of palace slum, attracting artists and craftsmen, its two most famous inhabitants being Nobel Prize-winning poet Jaroslav Seifert, and Franz Kafka, who came here in the evenings to write short stories during the winter of 1916.

Lobkowicz Palace (Lobkovický palác)

MAP PAGE 28, POCKET MAP D10
Jiřská 3. ⓦ lobkowicz.cz. Charge.

Appropriated in 1939 and again in 1948, and only handed back in the late 1990s, the **Lobkowicz Palace** now houses an impressive selection of the Lobkowicz family's prize possessions (with audio-guide accompaniment), including original manuscripts by Mozart and Beethoven, old musical instruments, arms and armour, and one or two masterpieces such as a Velázquez portrait, Pieter Brueghel the Elder's sublime *Haymaking* from the artist's famous cycle of seasons, and two views of London by Canaletto.

South Gardens (Jižní zahrady)

MAP PAGE 28, POCKET MAP C11

These gardens, which link up with the terraced gardens of Malá Strana (see page 45), enjoy wonderful vistas over the city. Originally laid out in the sixteenth century, the gardens were remodelled in the 1920s with the addition of an observation terrace and

South Gardens offers fine city views

colonnaded pavilion, beneath which is an earlier eighteenth-century *Hudební pavilón* (music pavilion). Two sandstone obelisks further east record the arrival of the two Catholic governors after their 1618 defenestration from the Royal Palace (see page 27).

Royal Gardens (Královská zahrada)

MAP PAGE 28, POCKET MAP C10

Founded by Ferdinand I in 1530, the **Royal Gardens** are smartly maintained, with fully functioning fountains and immaculately cropped lawns. It's a popular spot, though more a place for admiring the azaleas and almond trees than lounging around on the grass. Set into the south terrace – from which there are unrivalled views over to the cathedral – is the Renaissance **ball-game court** (Míčovna), occasionally used for concerts and exhibitions. The walls are tattooed with sgraffito and feature a hammer and sickle, thoughtfully added by restorers in the 1950s.

Prague Castle Picture Gallery (Obrazárna pražského hradu)

MAP PAGE 28, POCKET MAP C11
Second courtyard.
Ⓦ kulturanahrade.cz. Charge.

The remnants of the **Imperial Collection**, started by Rudolf

Belvedere, the city's finest Renaissance building

Prague Castle from the Royal Gardens

II, are housed here. Among the collection's finest paintings is Rubens' richly coloured *Assembly of the Gods at Olympus*, an illusionist triple portrait of Rudolf II and his Habsburg predecessors that's typical of the sort of tricksy work that appealed to the emperor. Elsewhere, there's an early, very beautiful *Young Woman at Her Toilet* by Titian, and Tintoretto's *Flagellation of Christ*, a late work in which the artist makes very effective and dramatic use of light.

Belvedere (Kralovský letohrádek)

MAP PAGE 28, POCKET MAP D10
Mariánské hradby 1.
Prague's most celebrated Renaissance building is a delicately

arcaded **summerhouse** topped by an inverted copper ship's hull, begun by Ferdinand I in 1538 for his wife, Anne (though she sadly didn't live long enough to see the design completed).

The Belvedere's exterior walls are decorated by a series of lovely figural reliefs depicting scenes from mythology, while the interior is normally in use as a beautiful venue for temporary exhibitions of contemporary art.

However, the main attraction here can be found outside in the palace's miniature formal garden – the **Singing Fountain**, which gets its name from the musical sound the droplets of water make when falling into the metal bowls below.

Restaurant

Villa Richter

MAP PAGE 28, POCKET MAP D10
Staré zámecké schody 6. ⓦ villarichter.cz.
Set scenically among the castle vineyards, just outside the Black Tower (Černá věž), *Villa Richter*

has three separate places one on top of the other: the *Piano Nobile* serves up classy duck, beef and seafood dishes; below, the *Piano Terra* specializes in Bohemian standards; and *Panorama Pergola* is the perfect place to sample some Czech wines while taking in the sublime views. KčKčKč

Hradčany

Hradčany – the district immediately outside Prague Castle – is replete with a string of ostentatious Baroque palaces built on an ever-increasing scale. The monumental appearance of these attention-stealing edifices is a direct result of the great fire of 1541, which destroyed the small-scale medieval houses that once stood here and allowed the Habsburg nobility to transform Hradčany into the grand architectural showpiece it still is. Nowadays, despite the steady stream of tourists en route to the castle, it's also one of the most peaceful enclaves in the city centre, barely disturbed by the army of civil servants who work in the area's numerous ministries and embassies. The three big-hitting attractions to make a beeline for are the Šternberg Palace, with its collection of Old Masters; the Baroque pilgrimage church of Loreto; and the ornate libraries of the Strahov Monastery.

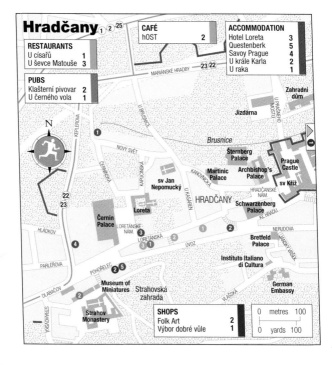

Hradčany ① ② ²⁵

RESTAURANTS
U císařů 1
U ševce Matouše 3

PUBS
Klášterní pivovar 2
U černého vola 1

CAFÉ
hOST 2

ACCOMMODATION
Hotel Loreta 3
Questenberk 5
Savoy Prague 4
U krále Karla 2
U raka 1

SHOPS
Folk Art 2
Výbor dobré vůle 1

0 metres 100
0 yards 100

MARIÁNSKÉ HRADBY 23 22

Zahradní dům

Jízdárna

KEPLEROVA

N

U BRUSNICE

Brusnice

NOVÝ SVĚT

ČERNÍNSKÁ

KAPUCÍNSKÁ

KANOVNICKÁ

Šternberg Palace

Martinic Palace

Archbishop's Palace

Prague Castle

sv Jan Nepomucký

U KASÁREN

HRADČANY

HRADČANSKÉ NÁM.

sv Kříž

Schwarzenberg Palace

U PRAŠNÉHO MOSTU

U PRAŠNÉHO MOSTU

KE HRADU

NERUDOVA

22 23

Černín Palace

Loreta

LORETÁNSKÉ NÁM.

LORETÁNSKÁ

ÚVOZ

Bretfeld Palace

Instituto Italiano di Cultura

LÁNSKÝ VRŠEK

HLÁDKOV

PARLÉŘOVA

POHOŘELEC

Museum of Miniatures

Strahovská zahrada

KLÁŠSKÁ

German Embassy

DLABAČOV

STRAHOVSKÁ

Strahov Monastery

Hradčanské náměstí is flanked by grand palaces

Hradčanské náměstí

MAP PAGE 34, POCKET MAP B11

Hradčanské náměstí (Hradcany Square) fans out from the castle gates, surrounded by the oversized palaces of the old Catholic nobility. The one spot everyone heads for is the ramparts in the southeastern corner, which allow an unrivalled view over the red rooftops of Malá Strana, and beyond. Few people make use of the square's central green patch, which is heralded by a wonderful giant green wrought-iron lamppost from the 1860s and, behind it, a Baroque plague column. The most noteworthy palaces on the square are the **Schwarzenberg Palace**, at no. 2, with its over-the-top sgraffito decoration, and the sumptuous, vanilla-coloured Rococo **Archbishop's Palace**, opposite.

Šternberg Palace

MAP PAGE 34, POCKET MAP B11

Hradčanské náměstí 15.

Ⓦ ngprague.cz. Charge.

The elegant, early eighteenth-century **Šternberg Palace** is now an art gallery housing **European Old Masters** from the fourteenth to the eighteenth century. It's a modest collection, though the handful of masterpieces makes a visit here worthwhile, and there's an elegant courtyard café. The ground floor contains several superb Cranach canvases, plus one of the most celebrated paintings in the whole collection: the *Feast of the Rosary* by Albrecht Dürer, one of Rudolf II's most prized acquisitions, which he had transported on foot across the Alps to Prague.

The highlights of the first floor include Dieric Bouts' *Lamentation*, a complex composition crowded with figures in medieval garb; two richly coloured Bronzino portraits; and Jan Gossaert's eye-catching *St Luke Drawing the Virgin*, an exercise in architectural geometry and perspective. Before you head upstairs, though, don't miss the side room (11) containing Orthodox icons from Venice, the Balkans and Russia.

The second floor boasts a searching portrait of old age by Tintoretto, a wonderfully rugged portrait by Goya and a mesmerizing *Praying Christ* by El Greco. Be sure to admire the Čínský kabinet, a small oval chamber smothered in gaudy Baroque Chinoiserie, and one of the palace's few surviving slices of original decor. Elsewhere, there is a series of canvases by the Brueghels, a Rembrandt, and Rubens' colossal *Murder of St Thomas* (room 30).

Schwarzenberg Palace

MAP PAGE 34, POCKET MAP B11
Hradčanské náměstí 2.
Ⓦ ngprague.cz. Charge.

The most outrageous, over-the-top, sgraffitoed pile on Hradčanské náměstí, **Schwarzenberg Palace** now shelters a collection of **Czech Baroque art**, of only limited interest to the non-specialist. Chronologically, you should begin on the second floor, where you get a brief glimpse of the overtly sensual and erotic Mannerist paintings that prevailed during the reign of Rudolf II (1576–1612). The rest of the gallery is given over to the art that spearheaded the Counter-Reformation in the Czech Lands: paintings by the likes of Bohemia's Karel Škréta and Petr Brandl, and the gesticulating sculptures of Matthias Bernhard Braun and Ferdinand Maximilian Brokof.

Martinic Palace

MAP PAGE 34, POCKET MAP B11
Hradčanské náměstí 8.

Compared to the other palaces on the square, the **Martinic Palace**

The Baroque facade of Loreto church

is a fairly modest pile, built in 1620 by one of the governors who survived the second defenestration (see page 29). Its rich sgraffito decoration, which continues in the inner courtyard, was only discovered during restoration work in the 1970s. On the facade, you can easily make out Potiphar's wife making a grab at a naked and unwilling Joseph. The interiors contain some exceptionally well-preserved Renaissance art as well as providing a glimpse of the lifestyle enjoyed by the palace's original owners. Lovely Late Renaissance painted ceilings and frescoes give new meaning to the term wall art, and there's a nice display of typical furnishings from the Renaissance era. Sadly, today it is only open during events.

Černín Palace

MAP PAGE 34, POCKET MAP A11
Loretánské náměstí 5. Closed to the public.

Loretánské náměstí is dominated by the phenomenal 135m-long facade of the **Černín Palace**, decorated with thirty Palladian half-columns and supported by a row of diamond-pointed rustication. Begun in the 1660s, the building nearly bankrupted future generations of the Černín

family, who were eventually forced to sell the palace to the Austrian state in 1851, which converted it into military barracks. Since 1918, the palace has housed the **Ministry of Foreign Affairs**, and during World War II it was, for a while, the Nazi Reichsprotektor's residence. On March 10, 1948, it was the scene of Prague's third – and most widely mourned – defenestration. Only days after the Communist coup, **Jan Masaryk**, the only son of the founder of Czechoslovakia, and the last remaining non-Communist in the cabinet, plunged to his death from the top-floor bathroom window of the palace.

Whether it was suicide (he had been suffering from bouts of depression, partly induced by the political developments in Czechoslovakia at the time) or murder will probably never be satisfactorily resolved, but for most people Masaryk's untimely death cast a dark shadow over the newly established regime. Jan Masaryk's story is the subject of a 2017 feature film, *A Prominent Patient*, which looks at his life and death and what he might have achieved had he lived longer.

Loreto

MAP PAGE 34, POCKET MAP A11
Loretánské náměstí 7. ⓦ loreta.cz. Charge.
The outer casing of the **Loreto** church was built in the early part of the eighteenth century – all hot flourishes and elaborate Baroque twirls, topped by a bell tower that clanks out the hymn "We Greet Thee a Thousand Times" on its 27 Dutch bells.

The focus of the pilgrimage complex is the **Santa Casa** (a mock-up of Mary's home in Nazareth), built in 1626 and smothered in a rich mantle of stucco depicting the building's miraculous transportation from the Holy Land. Pride of place within is given to a limewood statue of

Schwarzenberg Palace

the Black Madonna and Child, encased in silver.

Behind the Santa Casa, the much larger **Church of the Nativity** has a high cherub count, plenty of Baroque gilding and a lovely organ replete with music-making angels and putti. As in the church, most of the saints honoured in the **cloisters** are women. Without doubt, the weirdest of the lot is St Wilgefortis (Starosta in Czech), whose statue stands in the final chapel of the cloisters. Daughter of the king of Portugal, she was due to marry the king of Sicily, despite having taken a vow of virginity. God intervened and she grew a beard, whereupon the king of Sicily broke off the marriage and her father had her crucified. Wilgefortis thus became the patron saint of unhappily married women, and is depicted bearded on the cross (and easily mistaken for Christ in drag).

You can get an idea of the Loreto's serious financial backing in the church's **treasury**, whose master exhibit is a tasteless Viennese silver monstrance, studded with diamonds taken from the wedding dress of

Countess Kolovrat, who made the Loreto sole heir to her fortune.

Nový svět

MAP PAGE 34, POCKET MAP A11

Nestling in a shallow dip in the northwest corner of Hradčany, **Nový svět** provides a glimpse of life on a totally different scale. Similar in many ways to the Golden Lane in the Hrad – but without the crowds – this picturesque cluster of brightly coloured cottages is all that remains of Hradčany's medieval slums, painted up and sanitized in the late eighteenth and early nineteenth centuries.

Strahov Monastery

MAP PAGE 34, POCKET MAP A12
Strahovské nadvoří 1.
Ⓦ strahovmonastery.cz. Charge.

The Baroque entrance to the **Strahov Monastery** is topped by a statue of St Norbert, who founded the order in 1140 and whose relics were brought here in 1627. The church, which was remodelled in Baroque times, is well worth a peek for its colourful frescoes relating to St Norbert's life, but it's the monastery's two ornate Baroque **libraries** (*knihovny*) that are the real reason for visiting Strahov.

The **Philosophical Hall** has walnut bookcases so tall they almost touch the frescoes on the library's lofty ceiling, while the paintings

on the low-ceilinged **Theological Hall** are framed by wedding-cake-style stuccowork. Look out, too, for the collection of curios in the glass cabinets outside the library, which features shells, turtles, crabs, lobsters, dried-up sea monsters, butterflies, beetles and plastic fruit. There's even a pair of whales' penises displayed alongside a narwhal horn, harpoons and a model ship.

The monastery's curation of religious art, displayed in the **Strahov Gallery** (*obrazárna*) above the cloisters, contains one or two gems: a portrait of Emperor Rudolf II by his court painter, Hans von Aachen, plus a superb portrait of Rembrandt's elderly mother by Gerrit Dou.

Museum of Miniatures

MAP PAGE 34, POCKET MAP A12
Strahovské nadvoří 11.
Ⓦ muzeumminiatur.cz. Charge.

The (appropriately) dinky **Museum of Miniatures** displays forty or so works by the Russian **Anatoly Konenko**, including the smallest book in the world, a thirty-page edition of Chekhov's *Chameleon*. Among the other miracles of miniscule manufacture are the Lord's Prayer written on a human hair; a caravan of camels passing through the eye of a needle; and a flea bearing golden horseshoes, scissors, and a key and lock.

Strahov Monastery

Nový svět

Shops

Folk Art

MAP PAGE 34, POCKET MAP A12
Pohořelec 7.
Specializes in a variety of handcrafted textiles including tablecloths, scarves and purses.

Výbor dobré vůle

MAP PAGE 34, POCKET MAP D10
Zlatá ulička 19.
All the crafts in this tiny Hrad shop (ticket needed) are made by disabled children, and profits go to the Olga Havlová Foundation.

Café

HOST

MAP PAGE 34, POCKET MAP B11
Loretánská 15. Ⓦ restauranthost.cz.
Down an inconspicuous flight of steps off Loretánská, this well-hidden, glass-fronted restaurant has fine Malá Strana views, a mix of Czech and international mains and an affordable lunch menu. KčKč

Restaurants

U císařů (The Emperor)

MAP PAGE 34, POCKET MAP B11
Loretánská 5. Ⓦ ucisaru.cz.
Upmarket medieval place serving up hearty, meaty Czech dishes, as well as lighter plates like grilled fish or salads, plus a selection of vegetarian pasta dishes. KčKč

U ševce Matouše (The Cobbler Matouš)

MAP PAGE 34, POCKET MAP A11
Loretánské náměstí 4.
Ⓦ usevcematouse.cz.
Fried pork steak served with a heap of potato salad is the local speciality dished up in this former cobbler's, which is one of the few half-decent places to eat in the castle district. Kč

Pubs and bars

Klašterní pivovar (The Monastery Brewery)

MAP PAGE 34, POCKET MAP A12
Strahovské nádvoří 1.
Tourist-friendly monastic brewery, offering its own light and dark St Norbert beers and a menu of Czech pub food.

U černého vola (The Black Ox)

MAP PAGE 34, POCKET MAP A11
Loretánské náměstí 1.
Great traditional Prague pub doing a brisk business serving huge quantities of popular light beer Velkopopovický kozel to thirsty local workers and in-the-know tourists, soaked up with a few classic pub snacks.

Malá Strana

Malá Strana, Prague's picturesque "Little Quarter", sits beneath the castle and is in many ways the city's most entrancing area. Its many peaceful, often hilly, cobbled backstreets have changed very little since Mozart walked them during his frequent visits to Prague between 1787 and 1791. They conceal a whole host of quiet terraced gardens, as well as the wooded Petřín Hill, which together provide the perfect inner-city escape in the summer months. The Church of sv Mikuláš, by far the finest Baroque church in Prague, and the Museum Kampa, with its unrivalled collection of works by František Kupka, are the two major sights.

Malostranské náměstí

MAP PAGE 42, POCKET MAP D11

Malostranské náměstí, Malá Strana's arcaded main square, is dominated and divided in two by the Baroque church of sv Mikuláš (see opposite). Trams and cars wind their way across the cobbles below the church, regularly dodged by a procession of people marching up the hill to the castle. On the square's north side at no. 18, distinguished by its pair of little turrets and rather shocking facade painted in a pistachio and vanilla colour scheme, is the **dům Smiřických**, where, in 1618, the Protestant posse met to decide how to get rid of Emperor Ferdinand's gaggle of Catholic governors: whether to attack them with daggers, or, as they eventually attempted, to kill them by chucking them out of the

Malostranské náměstí is threaded by rattling trams

Malá Strana unfurls beneath the castle

window of the Old Royal Palace (see page 27).

Parliament

MAP PAGE 42, POCKET MAP D11
Sněmovna 4. ⓦ psp.cz.

The Czech parliament occupies a Neoclassical palace that served as the provincial Diet in the nineteenth century. Later it housed the National Assembly of the First Republic in 1918, the Czech National Council after federalization in 1968, and, since 1993, it has been home to the **Chamber of Deputies** (Poslanecká sněmovna), the (more important) lower house of the Czech parliament. To find out more, visit the **information centre** at Malostranské náměstí 6 (Mon–Fri 9am–4pm).

Church of sv Mikuláš

MAP PAGE 42, POCKET MAP C11–D12
Malostranské náměstí.
ⓦ stnicholas.cz. Charge.

Towering over the whole of Malá Strana is the Baroque **Church of sv Mikuláš** (St Nicholas), whose giant green dome and tower are among the most characteristic

landmarks on Prague's left bank. Built by the Jesuits in the early eighteenth century, it was their most ambitious project yet in Bohemia, and the ultimate symbol of their stranglehold on the country. Nothing about the relatively plain west facade prepares you for the overwhelming High Baroque interior. The vast fresco in the nave portrays some of the more fanciful miraculous feats of St Nicholas, while the dome at the east end of the church is even more impressive, thanks, more than anything, to its sheer height. Leering over you as you gaze up at the dome are four terrifyingly oversized and stern Church Fathers, one of whom brandishes a gilded thunderbolt, leaving no doubt as to the gravity of the Jesuit message. It's also possible to climb the **tower** (charge) for fine views over Malá Strana and Charles Bridge.

Nerudova

MAP PAGE 42, POCKET MAP C11

The busiest of the cobbled streets leading up to the castle is **Nerudova**. Historically, this was the city's main area

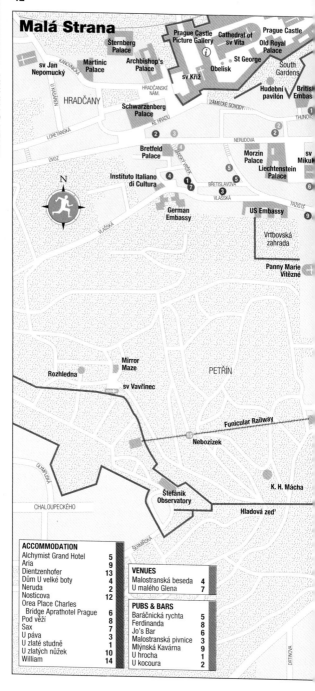

Malá Strana

Prague Castle Picture Gallery
Cathedral of sv Víta
Prague Castle Old Royal Palace

Šternberg Palace

sv Jan Nepomucký

Martinic Palace

Archbishop's Palace

St George

Obelisk

sv Kříž

South Gardens

HRADČANSKÉ NÁM.

HRADČANY

Schwarzenberg Palace

Hudební pavilón

British Embas

ZÁMECKÉ SCHODY

LORETÁNSKÁ

Bretfeld Palace

NERUDOVA

Morzin Palace

sv Miku

ÚVOZ

Instituto Italiano di Cultura

Liechtenstein Palace

BŘETISLAVOVA

VLAŠSKÁ

N

German Embassy

US Embassy

Vrtbovská zahrada

Panny Marie Vítězné

VLAŠSKÁ

Mirror Maze

Rozhledna

sv Vavřinec

PETŘÍN

Funicular Railway

Nebozízek

K. H. Mácha

OLYMPIJSKÁ

CHALOUPECKÉHO

Štefánik Observatory

Hladová zeď'

ŠERMÍŘSKÁ

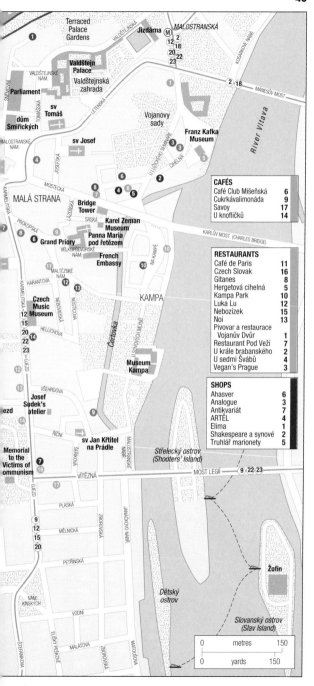

CAFÉS

Café Club Míšeňská	6
Cukrkávalimonáda	9
Savoy	17
U knoflíčků	14

RESTAURANTS

Café de Paris	11
Czech Slovak	16
Gitanes	8
Hergetová cihelná	5
Kampa Park	10
Luka Lu	12
Nebozízek	15
Noi	13
Pivovar a restaurace Vojanův Dvůr	1
Restaurant Pod Veží	7
U krále brabanského	2
U sedmi Švábů	4
Vegan's Prague	3

SHOPS

Ahasver	6
Analogue	3
Antikvariát	7
ARTĚL	4
Elima	1
Shakespeare a synové	2
Truhlář marionety	5

for craftspeople, artisans and artists, though the shops and restaurants that line Nerudova now are mostly aimed at tourists. Many of the houses retain their medieval barn doors and peculiar pictorial house signs. One of Nerudova's fancier buildings, at no. 5, is the **Morzin Palace**, now the Romanian Embassy, its doorway supported by two Moors (a pun on the owner's name). Meanwhile, opposite, two giant eagles hold up the portal of the **Thun-Hohenštejn Palace**, now the Italian Embassy. Further up the street, according to legend, Casanova and Mozart are said to have met up at a ball given by the aristocrat owners of no. 33, the Bretfeld Palace.

Valdštejn Palace

MAP PAGE 42, POCKET MAP D11
Valdštejnské náměstí 4. Ⓦ senat.cz.
Built in the 1620s for Albrecht von Waldstein, commander of the Imperial Catholic armies of the Thirty Years' War, the **Valdštejn Palace** was one of the first and largest Baroque palaces in the city. Nowadays, it houses the Czech

parliament's upper house, or **Senate** (Senát), whose sumptuous Baroque chambers can be visited on a tour at the weekend in warmer months.

Karel Zeman Museum

MAP PAGE 42, POCKET MAP D12
Saská 3. Ⓦ muzeumkarlazemana.cz.
Charge.
Czech animator, director and special effects innovator **Karel Zeman** influenced a generation of filmmakers and technicians, from George Lucas and Steven Spielberg to Tim Burton and Terry Gilliam. This museum covers the director's entire filmography. Exhibits detail the **special effects** techniques used in individual movies, each accompanied by a video showcasing their use. Best of all is the interactive nature of the museum: visitors can record themselves in front of a rear-projected image or film a shoot through a 3D model.

Valdštejnská zahrada (Palace Gardens)

MAP PAGE 42, POCKET MAP D11
Letenská 123/4.
Valdštejn Palace's **formal gardens** are accessible from the palace's

Valdštejn Palace houses the Senate

main entrance, and also from a doorway in the palace walls along Letenská. The focus is a gigantic Italianate **sala terrena**, a monumental loggia decorated with frescoes of the Trojan Wars, which stands at the end of an avenue of sculptures. In addition, there are freely roaming peacocks, a pseudo grotto along the south wall, with quasi-stalactites, and an aviary of eagle owls.

Terraced Palace Gardens

MAP PAGE 42, POCKET MAP D10
Valdštejnská. Charge.

A great way to reach the Hrad is via Malá Strana's Baroque **Terraced Palace Gardens**, draped across the steep slopes where the royal vineyards used to be. Dotted with urns and statuary, they command superb views over Prague. From Valdštejnská, you enter via the Ledeburská zahrada, gardens which connect higher up with the castle's own South Gardens (see page 31).

Franz Kafka Museum

MAP PAGE 42, POCKET MAP E11
Cihelná 2b. ⓦ kafkamuseum.cz. Charge.

This **museum** offers a fairly sophisticated rundown of the life and works of the Czech–German writer **Franz Kafka** (1883–1924). The first section includes photos of the old ghetto into which Kafka was born; an invoice from his father's shop, with the logo of a jackdaw (*kavka* in Czech); copies of his job applications, requests for sick leave; one of his reports on accident prevention in the workplace; and facsimiles of his pen sketches.

Upstairs, audiovisuals and theatrical trickery are used to explore the torment, alienation and claustrophobia Kafka felt throughout his life and expressed in his writings. On a lighter note, don't miss David Černý's *Pissing Figures* (*Čůrající postavy*) statue holding centre stage in the

Church of sv Mikuláš

courtyard outside, which features two men urinating into a pool shaped like the Czech Republic.

Maltézské náměstí

MAP PAGE 42, POCKET MAP D12
Maltézské náměstí is one of a clutch of delightful little squares between Karmelitská and the river. At the north end is a plague column, topped by a statue of St John the Baptist, but the square takes its name from the Order of the Knights of St John of Jerusalem (now known as the Maltese Knights). In 1160, they founded the nearby church of **Panna Maria pod řetězem** (St Mary below-the-chain), so-called because it was the Knights' responsibility to guard the Judith Bridge (predecessor to Charles Bridge).

Only two bulky Gothic towers are still standing, and the apse is now thoroughly Baroque, but the nave remains unfinished and open to the elements.

John Lennon Wall

MAP PAGE 42, POCKET MAP D12
The pretty little square of **Velkopřevorské náměstí** echoes

to the sound of music from the nearby Prague conservatoire, its northern limit marked by the garden wall of the Grand Priory of the Maltese Knights. Here, following John Lennon's death in 1980, Prague's youth established an ad hoc shrine smothered in graffiti tributes to the ex-Beatle. The running battle between police and graffiti artists continued well into the 1990s, with the society of Maltese Knights taking an equally dim view of the mural, but a compromise has now been reached and the wall's scribblings legalized. While you're in the vicinity, be sure to check out the love padlocks which have been secured to the railings of the nearby bridge.

Kampa

MAP PAGE 42, POCKET MAP D13–E12
Heading for **Kampa**, the largest of the Vltava's islands, with its cafés, old mills and serene riverside park, is the perfect way to escape the crowds. The island is separated from the left bank by Prague's "Little Venice", a thin strip of water called **Čertovka** (Devil's Stream), which used

John Lennon Wall pays homage to the icon

to power several millwheels until the last one ceased to function in 1936. For much of its history, the island was the city's main washhouse area, a fact commemorated by the church of **sv Jan Křtitel na Prádle** (St John-the-Baptist at the Cleaners) on Říční. It wasn't until the sixteenth and seventeenth centuries that the Nostitz family, who owned Kampa, began to develop the northern half of the island; the southern half was left untouched, and today is laid out as a public park, with riverside views across to Staré Město. To the north, the oval main square, **Na Kampě**, once a pottery market, is studded with slender acacia trees and cut through by Charles Bridge, to which it is connected by a double flight of steps.

Throughout Kampa, look out for the high-water marks from the devastating flood of 2002 – water reached first-floor rooms here.

Museum Kampa

MAP PAGE 42, POCKET MAP D13–E13
U Sovových mlýnů 2.
Ⓦ museumkampa.cz. Charge.
Housed in an old riverside watermill, **Museum Kampa** is dedicated to the private art collection of Jan and Meda Mládek. As well as temporary exhibitions, the stylish modern gallery also shelters the best of the Mládeks' collection, including a whole series of works by the Czech artist **František Kupka**, seen by many as the father of abstract art. These range from early Expressionist watercolours to transitional pastels like *Fauvist Chair* from 1910, and more abstract works, such as the seminal oil painting, *Cathedral and Study for Fugue in Two Colours*, from around 1912. The gallery also displays a good selection of Cubist and later interwar works by the sculptor **Otto Gutfreund** and a few collages by postwar surrealist Jiří Kolář.

David Černý's *Pissing Figures* sculpture outside the Franz Kafka Museum

Vrtbovská zahrada

MAP PAGE 42, POCKET MAP C12
Karmelitská 25. ⓦ vrtbovska.cz. Charge.
One of the most elusive of Malá
Strana's many Baroque gardens, the
Vrtbovská zahrada was founded
on the site of the former vineyards
of the Vrtbov Palace. Laid out on
Tuscan-style terraces, dotted with
ornamental urns and statues of
the gods by Matthias Bernhard
Braun, the gardens twist their way
up the lower slopes of Petřín Hill
to an observation terrace from
where there's a spectacular rooftop
perspective on the city.

Church of Panny Marie Vítězné

MAP PAGE 42, POCKET MAP C12–D12
Karmelitská 9. ⓦ pragjesu.info.
Surprisingly, given its rather plain
exterior (it started life as a German
Protestant church), the **Church of
Panny Marie Vítězné** (Our Lady
of Victory) houses a high-kitsch
wax effigy of the infant Jesus as a
precocious 3-year-old, enthroned
in a glass case. Attributed with
miraculous powers, this image,
known as the **Bambino di Praga**
(or Prazské Jezulátko), became an
object of international pilgrimage
and continues to attract visitors,
mainly Catholics from southern
Europe and Poland. The *bambino*
boasts a vast personal wardrobe
of expensive swaddling clothes –
approaching a hundred separate
outfits at the last count – regularly
changed by the Carmelite nuns.
A small number of these outfits is
on display in a miniscule museum,
which can be found up the
spiral staircase in the south aisle,
including a selection of his velvet
and satin overgarments sent from
all over the world.

Czech Music Museum

MAP PAGE 42, POCKET MAP D12–D13
Karmelitská 2. ⓦ nm.cz. Charge.
Set in a former nunnery, the
permanent collection of the **Czech
Music Museum** (České muzeum
hudby) begins with a crazy cut-
and-splice medley of musical film
footage from the last century.
Next up is August Förster's
pioneering quarter-tone grand
piano from 1924 – you can even
listen to Alois Hába's microtonal

Fantazie no. 10, composed for, and performed on, its three keyboards. After this rather promising start, the museum settles down into a conventional display of old central European instruments, from a precious Baumgartner clavichord and an Amati violin to Neapolitan mandolins and a vast contrabass over 2m in height. Best of all is the fact that you can hear many of the instruments on display being put through their paces at listening posts in each room.

Josef Sudek's Atelier

MAP PAGE 42, POCKET MAP D13
Újezd 30. ⓦ sudek-atelier.cz. Charge.
Hidden behind the buildings on the east side of the Újezd is a faithful reconstruction of the cute little wooden garden studio, where **Josef Sudek** (1896–1976), the great Czech photographer, lived with his sister from 1927. Sudek moved out in 1958, but he used the place as his darkroom to the end of his life. The twisted tree in the front garden will be

familiar to those acquainted with the numerous photographic cycles he based around the studio. The building itself has only a few of Sudek's personal effects and is now used for temporary exhibitions of other photographers' works.

Memorial to the Victims of Communism

MAP PAGE 42, POCKET MAP D14
Újezd/Vítězná.
In 2002, the Czechs finally erected a **Memorial to the Victims of Communism**. The location has no particular resonance with the period, but the memorial itself has an eerie quality, especially when illuminated at night. It consists of a series of statues and self-portraits by sculptor **Olbram Zoubek**, standing on steps leading down from Petřín Hill behind, each in varying stages of disintegration. The inscription at the base of the monument reads "205,486 convicted, 248 executed, 4500 died in prison, 327 annihilated at the border, 170,938 emigrated".

Rozhledna, Petřín's take on the Eiffel Tower

Petřín

MAP PAGE 42, POCKET MAP A13–C13

The hilly wooded slopes of **Petřín**, distinguished by the Rozhledna (see page 49), a scaled-down version of the Eiffel Tower, make up the largest green space in the city centre. The tower is just one of several exhibits which survive from the **1891 Prague Exhibition**, whose modest legacy also includes the hill's funicular railway. At the top of the hill, it's possible to trace the southernmost perimeter wall of the old city, popularly known as the **Hunger Wall** (Hladová zeď). Instigated in the 1460s by Emperor Charles IV, it was much lauded at the time as a great public work which provided employment for the burgeoning ranks of the city's destitute (hence its name); in fact, much of the wall's construction was paid for by the expropriation of Jewish property.

Funicular railway

MAP PAGE 42, POCKET MAP B13–C13

The **funicular railway** (lanová dráha) up to Petřín departs from a station just off Újezd and runs every 10–15min; ordinary public transport tickets and travel passes are valid on the service. At the Nebozízek stop halfway up, where the carriages pass each other, you can get out and soak up the spectacular view at the *Nebozízek (Little Auger) restaurant* (see page 52); the top station is closest to the Mirror Maze and Rozhledna.

Though the journey is only 510m long, and lasts just a few minutes, it saves your legs a lot of effort.

Štefánik Observatory

MAP PAGE 42, POCKET MAP B14–C14
Ⓦ observatory.cz. Charge.

At the top of the hill, the Hunger Wall (see page 49) runs southeast from the funicular to Petřín's **Štefánik Observatory**. The small astronomical exhibition inside is hardly worth bothering with, but if it's a clear night, a quick peek

The funicular trundles up Petřín

through either of the observatory's two powerful telescopes is a treat.

Rozhledna

MAP PAGE 42, POCKET MAP B13
Ⓦ petrinska-rozhledna.cz. Charge.

Petřín's most familiar landmark is **Rozhledna**, a miniature, octagonal version of the Eiffel Tower, a mere fifth of the size of the original. It was built after members of the Czech Hiking Club visited Paris in 1889 – so taken were they with the Paris tower that they decided to build a copy in Prague. Many see it as a tribute to the city's strong cultural and political links with Paris at the time. The view from the public gallery is the best in the city.

Mirror Maze (Bludiště)

MAP PAGE 42, POCKET MAP B13
Ⓦ petrinska-rozhledna.cz. Charge.

The **Mirror Maze** is housed in a mini neo-Gothic castle complete with mock drawbridge. There is also an action-packed, life-sized **diorama** of the victory of Prague's students and Jews over the Swedes on Charles Bridge in 1648. Great fun for both adults and kids.

Shops

Ahasver
MAP PAGE 42, POCKET MAP D12
Prokopská 3.
A delightful little shop selling antique gowns and jewellery, as well as paintings, porcelain and glass.

Analogue
MAP PAGE 42, POCKET MAP C12
Vlašská 10.
The future is analogue at this tiny temple to all things non-digital, where the speciality is film photography.

Antikvariát
MAP PAGE 42, POCKET MAP D13
Újezd 26.
Small secondhand bookshop crammed with tomes, which also sells old film and theatre posters.

ARTĚL
MAP PAGE 42, POCKET MAP D12
U lužického semináře 7.
Specializing in handcrafted Bohemian crystal glassware, the shop is a treasure trove of unique pieces decorated with lovely motifs.

Shakespeare a synové

Elima
MAP PAGE 42, POCKET MAP C12
Janský vršek 5.
This miniscule shop tucked away in the backstreets sells a careful curation of beautiful, inexpensive, handmade Polish pottery from Boleslawiec (Bunzlau).

Shakespeare a synové
MAP PAGE 42, POCKET MAP E12
U lužického semináře 10.
Don't be deceived by the tiny frontage; this is a wonderful, large, rambling and well-stocked English-language bookstore. A perfect spot in which to while away some time.

Truhlář marionety
MAP PAGE 42, POCKET MAP D12
U lužického semináře 5.
Prague is awash with cheap, and frankly quite gawdy, puppets, but the Truhlář family's designs are a cut above the rest.

Cafés

Café Club Míšeňská
MAP PAGE 42, POCKET MAP D12
Míšeňská 71/3.
Ⓦ facebook.com/misenskafe.
A relaxed and hidden-away spot for great coffee and delicious cheesecake in what is otherwise a very busy area. Also serves up a small menu of hot and cold savoury snacks. Kč

Cukrkávalimonáda
MAP PAGE 42, POCKET MAP D12
Lázeňská 7. Ⓦ cukrkavalimonada.com.
Very professional and well-run café serving good brasserie-style dishes, as well as coffee and croissants, with tables overlooking the church of Panna Maria pod řetězem. Kč

Savoy
MAP PAGE 42, POCKET MAP D14
Vítězná 5. Ⓦ cafesavoy.ambi.cz/en.
An L-shaped Habsburg-era café from 1893 with a superb, neo-Renaissance ceiling; you can just

Savoy café

have a coffee or a snack if you want, but it doubles as a very good restaurant, with mains (including lots of seafood) Kč

Restaurants

Café de Paris

MAP PAGE 42, POCKET MAP D12
Maltezské náměstí 4. Ⓦ cafedeparis.cz/cs.
A cosy family-run restaurant based on Geneva's famous *Café de Paris*. The signature dish is beef entrecôte in a creamy sauce made from a secret recipe. KčKčKč

Czech Slovak

MAP PAGE 42, POCKET MAP D14
Újezd 20. Ⓦ czechslovak.cz.
Upmarket return to the halcyon days of Czechoslovak cuisine with its twenty first-century white and black decor, up-lit in neon purple, and traditional menu. KčKčKčKč

Gitanes

MAP PAGE 42, POCKET MAP C12
Tržiště 7. ☏ 257 530 163.
A surreal dining space in which to feast on well-executed Mediterranean food inspired by Dalmatian and Montenegrin flavours and recipes. KčKč

Hergetová cihelná

MAP PAGE 42, POCKET MAP E11
Cihelná 2b. ☏ 296 826 103.
Slick restaurant serving Tiger prawn starters, plus pasta and risotto, and the odd traditional Czech dish. The riverside summer terrace overlooks Charles Bridge. KčKč

Kampa Park

MAP PAGE 42, POCKET MAP E12
Na Kampě 8b. Ⓦ kampapark.com.
Pink house exquisitely located right by the Vltava on Kampa Island, with a superb fish and seafood menu, top-class service and tables outside in summer. KčKčKčKč

Luka Lu

MAP PAGE 42, POCKET MAP D13
Újezd 33. Ⓦ lukalu.cz.
This Serb restaurant does a good line in grilled Balkan meat dishes, while touting for the 'most colourful Prague restaurant' award, its art-filled walls competing with floorboards, ceilings, furnishings and fittings painted in the brightest of hues. KčKčKč

Nebozízek (Little Auger)

MAP PAGE 42, POCKET MAP C13
Petřínské sady 411.
Ⓦ nebozizek.cz/restaurace.
Situated at the halfway stop on the
Petřín funicular, *Nebozízek* offers
superb views – best taken in from
the outdoor terrace. A traditional
Czech menu features lots of game
dishes. KčKčKč

Noi

MAP PAGE 42, POCKET MAP D13
Újezd 19. Ⓦ noirestaurant.cz.
A stylish, atmospheric restaurant
dishing out some of the tastiest,
spiciest Thai food in Prague, with a
good plant-based menu for vegans
and vegetarians. There's a lovely
courtyard round the back. KčKč

Pivovar a restaurace Vojanův Dvůr

MAP PAGE 42, POCKET MAP E11
U Lužického semináře 21. Ⓦ vojanuvdvur.cz.
A cosy spot that's great for classic
Czech specialities like confit duck
leg with roasted potato dumplings
or pork ribs marinated in beer. It
also dishes up salads, pastas and
burgers and offers a good selection
of beer. KčKč

Restaurant Pod Věží

Restaurant Pod Věží

MAP PAGE 42, POCKET MAP D12
Mostecká 58/2. Ⓦ restaurantpodvezi.com.
This restaurant is attached to the
hotel *Pod Věží* (see page 123) and
serves a refined French-inspired
menu paired with a fantastic wine
list. KčKčKč

U krále brabantského

MAP PAGE 42, POCKET MAP C11
Thunovská 198/15. Ⓦ krcmabrabant.cz.
This rough, medieval tavern –
which claims to be Prague's oldest
– has been serving platters of meat
and jugs of ale to jovial patrons
since 1375. Everyone from King
Václav IV to Jaroslav Hášek is said
to have eaten in this unassuming
little restaurant. KčKčKč

U sedmi Švábů (The Seven Swabians)

MAP PAGE 42, POCKET MAP C11
Janský vršek 241. Ⓦ 7svabu.cz.
Named after the Grimm brothers'
tale, this atmospheric torch-lit
tavern serves up traditional Czech
beer and food to the occasional
accompaniment of medieval
shenanigans, from fire breathing to
sword fighting. KčKčKč

Vegan's Prague

MAP PAGE 42, POCKET MAP C11
Nerudova 221. Ⓦ vegansprague.cz.
Offering a vegan twist on
traditional Czech dishes, *Vegan's
Prague* is a great way to taste local
delicacies without the meat. Try the
cabbage goulash with dumplings
or opt for a plant-based take on
svíčková (hearty Czech meat stew
with dumplings). There's also a
decent selection of burgers and
salads on offer. Kč

Pubs and bars

Baráčnická rychta

MAP PAGE 42, POCKET MAP C12
Na tržišti 23. Ⓦ baracnickarychta.cz.
Všebaráčnická rychta (as it's also
known) is a nostalgia-inducing,

wood-panelled old beer hall dedicated to keeping things traditionally Czech in the heart of Malá Strana. One of the few 1930s Modernist buildings to be found in the area.

Ferdinanda

MAP PAGE 42, POCKET MAP C12
Karmelitská 18. Ⓦ ferdinanda.cz.
The Ferdinand brewery's second pub in Prague has four brews on tap (both its dark and the pale lager 11° are delicious). There's a good lunch menu, too, and a sociable atmosphere among patrons.

Jo's Bar

MAP PAGE 42, POCKET MAP C12
Malostranské náměstí 7.
Ⓦ cafescholz.cz.
Jo's is the city's original American backpacker hangout. Though it no longer has quite the same vitality, it remains a good place to meet other travellers. There's a club downstairs.

Malostranská pivnice

MAP PAGE 42, POCKET MAP E11
Cihelná 3. Ⓦ malostranskapivnice.cz.
Be warned: tourists are spotted a mile away, but for excellent Pilsner, as well as dark Kozel beers in a quiet courtyard, this *pivnice* is hard to beat.

Mlýnská kavárna

MAP PAGE 42, POCKET MAP D13
Všehrdova 14 (entry from Kampa Park).
This quiet spot on Kampa Island attracts journalists, politicians and artists, all hanging out around a rough wooden table, at the large bar, or on the terrace.

U hrocha (The Hippopotamus)

MAP PAGE 42, POCKET MAP C11
Thunovská 10. Ⓣ 257 533 389.
A close-knit bunch of locals fills out this small, smoky Czech *pivnice*, which is located close to the British Embassy and serves Pilsner Urquell.

Malostranská beseda

U kocoura (The Cat)

MAP PAGE 42, POCKET MAP D11
Nerudova 2. Ⓣ 257 530 107.
The most famous Czech pub on Nerudova inevitably attracts tourists, but the locals come here too for the Pilsner Urquell and Budvar, plus the obvious Czech stomach-fillers.

Venues

Malostranská beseda

MAP PAGE 42, POCKET MAP D11
Malostranské náměstí 21.
Ⓦ malostranska-beseda.cz.
This authentically Czech venue started life as Malá Strana's original town hall, a function it served until 1748. Refurbished a decade ago, it's one of the best places to catch local rock and big beat bands, from both Prague and the countryside.

U malého Glena (Little Glenn's)

MAP PAGE 42, POCKET MAP D12
Karmelitská 23. Ⓦ malyglen.cz.
The tiny downstairs stage at *U Malého Glena* hosts an eclectic mix of Latin jazz, bebop and blues.

Staré Město

Staré Město – literally the "Old Town" – is Prague's most central, vital ingredient. The busiest restaurants and pubs are here, and during the day a gaggle of shoppers and tourists fills its complex and utterly confusing web of narrow byways. Yet despite all the commercial activity, there are still plenty of residential streets, giving the area a lived-in feel rarely found in European city centres. At the heart of the district is the Old Town Square (Staroměstské náměstí), Prague's showpiece main square, easily the most magnificent in central Europe, and a great place to get your bearings before heading off into the labyrinthine backstreets. The best approach is from the city's most famous medieval landmark, the statue-encrusted Charles Bridge.

Charles Bridge (Karlův most)

MAP PAGE 56, POCKET MAP E12

Bristling with statuary and crowded with people, **Charles Bridge** is by far the city's most famous monument. Built in the fourteenth century by Charles IV, the bridge originally featured just a simple crucifix. The first sculpture wasn't added until 1683, when **St John of Nepomuk** appeared. His statue was such a propaganda success that the Catholic church authorities ordered another 21 to be erected between 1706 and 1714. Individually, only a few of the works are outstanding, but taken collectively, set against

Church of sv František z Assisi

The city's iconic Charles Bridge

the backdrop of the Hrad, the effect is breathtaking.

The bridge is now one of the city's most popular places to hang out, from dawn til dusk: the crush of sightseers never abates during the day, when the niches created by the bridge-piers are occupied by souvenir-hawkers and buskers, but after dark things calm down a bit, and the views are, if anything, even more spectacular.

You can climb both of the mighty Gothic **bridge towers** for a bird's-eye view of the masses pouring across. The one on the Malá Strana side (charge) features two unequal towers, connected by a castellated arch, which forms the entrance to the bridge. The Staré Město one (charge) is arguably the finer of the two, its eastern facade still encrusted in Gothic cake-like decorations from Peter Parler's workshop.

Church of sv František z Assisi (St Francis of Assisi)

MAP PAGE 56, POCKET MAP F12
Křížovnické náměstí.
Built in the 1680s for the Czech Order of Knights of the Cross

with a Red Star (the original gatekeepers of the bridge), the interior of the half-brick **Church of sv František z Assisi** is covered in rich marble and gilded furnishings and dominated by its huge dome, decorated with a sprawling fresco of *The Last Judgement* and luxurious marble furnishings.

Charles Bridge Museum (Muzeum Karlova mostu)

MAP PAGE 56, POCKET MAP F12
Křížovnické náměstí 3.
ⓦ muzeumkarlovamostu.cz. Charge.
Those with an interest in stone masonry and engineering will enjoy the exhibition; everyone else will probably get more out of the archive film footage.

Church of sv Salvátor (St Saviour)

MAP PAGE 56, POCKET MAP F12
Křížovnické náměstí.
The facade of the **Church of sv Salvátor** prickles with saintly statues which are lit up attractively at night. Founded in 1593, it marks the beginning of the Jesuits' rise to power and is part of the Klementinum (see page 58).

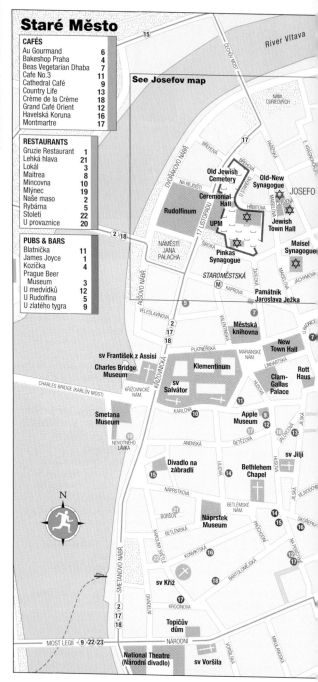

Staré Město

CAFÉS

Au Gourmand	6
Bakeshop Praha	4
Beas Vegetarian Dhaba	7
Cafe No.3	11
Cathedral Café	9
Country Life	13
Crème de la Crème	18
Grand Café Orient	12
Havelská Koruna	16
Montmartre	17

RESTAURANTS

Gruzie Restaurant	1
Lehká hlava	21
Lokál	3
Maitrea	8
Mincovna	10
Mlýnec	19
Naše maso	2
Rybárna	5
Stoleti	22
U provaznice	20

PUBS & BARS

Blatnička	11
James Joyce	1
Kozička	4
Prague Beer Museum	3
U medvídků	12
U Rudolfina	5
U zlatého tygra	9

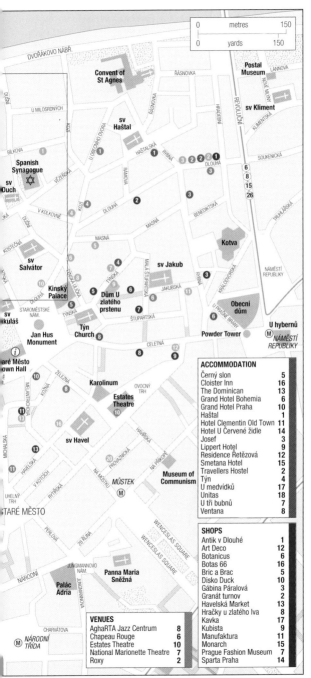

ACCOMMODATION	
Černý slon	5
Cloister Inn	16
The Dominican	13
Grand Hotel Bohemia	6
Grand Hotel Praha	10
Haštal	1
Hotel Clementin Old Town	11
Hotel U Červené židle	14
Josef	3
Lippert Hotel	9
Residence Řetězová	12
Smetana Hotel	15
Travellers Hostel	2
Týn	4
U medvídků	17
Unitas	18
U tří bubnů	7
Ventana	8

SHOPS	
Antik v Dlouhé	1
Art Deco	12
Botanicus	6
Botas 66	16
Bric a Brac	5
Disko Duck	10
Gábina Páralová	3
Granát turnov	2
Havelská Market	13
Hračky u zlatého Iva	8
Kavka	17
Kubista	9
Manufaktura	11
Monarch	15
Prague Fashion Museum	7
Sparta Praha	14

VENUES	
AghaRTA Jazz Centrum	8
Chapeau Rouge	6
Estates Theatre	10
National Marionette Theatre	7
Roxy	2

Like many Jesuit churches, its design copies that of the Gesù church in Rome; it's worth a quick look, if only for the frothy stucco plasterwork and delicate ironwork in its triple-naved interior.

Karlova

MAP PAGE 56, POCKET MAP F12
As the quickest route between Charles Bridge and the Old Town Square, the narrow street of **Karlova** is packed with people day and night, their attention divided between the souvenir shops and not losing their way as the street zigzags to the river. With Europop blaring from several shops, jesters' hats and puppets in abundance, and heaps of dubious jewellery on offer, the whole atmosphere can be a bit oppressive in the height of summer – a more peaceful alternative is to head through the Klementinum's courtyards.

Klementinum

MAP PAGE 56, POCKET MAP F12
Karlova 1. ⓦ klementinum.com. Charge.
Few people notice the **former Jesuit College** on the north side of Karlova, despite it covering a

Karlova is a bustling thoroughfare

huge area second in size only to the castle. The Habsburg rulers summoned the Jesuits to Prague in 1556 to help bolster the Catholic cause in Bohemia, and put them in charge of the entire education system, only to expel them in 1773. The complex now belongs to the state and Charles University, and shelters, among other things, the **National Library**. Aside from the ornate **Mirrored Chapel** (Zrcadlová kaple), a choice classical music venue, the Klementinum's most easily accessible attractions are open to the public on a 45-minute **guided tour** (in English).

The most spectacular sight is the **Baroque Library**, a long room lined with leather tomes, whose ceiling is decorated with one continuous illusionistic fresco praising secular wisdom, and whose wrought-iron gallery balustrade is held up by wooden barley-sugar columns. Upstairs, at roughly the centre of the **Klementinum** complex, is the **Astronomical Tower**, from which there's a superb view over central Prague. The weather has been recorded here since 1775, one of the world's longest periods of continual meteorological observation.

Apple Museum

MAP PAGE 56, POCKET MAP F12
Husova 21.
ⓦ applemuseum360.com. Charge.
Located just off Karlova, the medieval lanes of Prague's Old Town provide an unlikely location for one of the world's most forward-thinking computer technology museums. Established in 2015 using items from private collections, the **Apple Museum** is unmissable, even for those with an aversion to Macs, iPads and iPhones. Guided – aptly enough – by your smartphone, the exhibition is the definitive Apple collection, with everything from Steve Jobs' New Balance trainers and the very first Apple I computer to chunky

The incredible Baroque Library in the Klementinum

1990s printers and a section on Pixar, founded by Jobs in 1986.

New Town Hall (Nová radnice)

MAP PAGE 56, POCKET MAP F12–G12
Mariánské náměstí 2.

The most striking features of the rather severe **New Town Hall** are the two gargantuan Art Nouveau statues which stand guard at either corner of the building. The one on the left, looking a bit like Darth Vader, is the "Iron Knight", mascot of the armourers' guild; to the right is the caricatured sixteenth-century Jewish sage and scholar, **Rabbi Löw**. According to legend, Löw was visited by Death on several occasions, but escaped his clutches until he reached the ripe old age of 97, when the Grim Reaper hid in a rose innocently given to him by his granddaughter. He is also credited with creating the Golem, a mute Frankenstein's monster type of figure, which periodically ran amok in Prague (see page 77). Since 1945, the building has been the seat and official residence of the mayor of Prague.

Malé náměstí

MAP PAGE 56, POCKET MAP G12
A little cobbled square at the eastern end of Karlova, **Malé náměstí** was originally settled by French merchants in the twelfth century and is home to the city's first apothecary, **U zlaté koruny** (The Golden Crown), opened by a Florentine in 1353 at no. 13. Boasting beautiful chandeliers and a restored Baroque interior, it's now a jewellery shop. Nearby is the russet-red, neo-Renaissance **Rott Haus**, originally an ironmonger's store founded by V.J. Rott in 1840. Its facade is smothered in agricultural scenes and motifs inspired by the Czech artist Mikuláš Aleš. At the centre of the square stands a (disused) fountain dating from 1560 which retains its beautiful, original wrought-iron canopy.

Smetana Museum (Muzeum Bedřicha Smetany)

MAP PAGE 56, POCKET MAP E12–F12
Novotného lávka 1. Ⓦ nm.cz. Charge.
Housed in a gaily decorated neo-Renaissance building on the

riverfront, the **Smetana Museum** celebrates the life and work of the most nationalist of all the great Czech composers, Bedřich Smetana. His greatest success was *The Bartered Bride*, which marked the birth of Czech opera, but he was forced to give up conducting in 1874 with the onset of deafness, and eventually died of syphilis in a mental health hospital. Unfortunately, the museum fails to capture much of the spirit of the man, though the views across to the castle are good.

Clam-Gallas Palace (Clam-gallasův palác)
MAP PAGE 56, POCKET MAP F12–G12
Mariánské náměstí 2.
Despite its size, the **Clam-Gallas Palace** is easy to overlook in a narrow space. It's a typically lavish Baroque affair, with big and burly *Atlantes* supporting the portals. Doors open only for concerts, with regular performances in the Opera Barocca series (Ⓦoperabarocca.cz).

Staroměstské náměstí (Old Town Square)
MAP PAGE 56, POCKET MAP G11–G12
Easily the most spectacular square in Prague, **Staroměstské náměstí**

is the traditional heart of the city. Most of the brightly coloured houses look eighteenth century, but their Baroque facades conceal considerably older buildings.

Over the centuries, the square has seen its fair share of demonstrations and battles: the **27 white crosses** set into the paving commemorate the Protestant leaders who were condemned to death on the orders of the Habsburg Emperor in 1621, while the patch of green grass marks the neo-Gothic east wing of the town hall, burned down by the Nazis on the final day of the Prague Uprising in May 1945.

Today, the square is lined with café tables in summer and packed with a Christmas market in winter, while tourists pour in all year round to watch the town hall's astronomical clock chime and to drink in the atmosphere of this historic showpiece.

Staré Město Town Hall (Staroměstská radnice)
MAP PAGE 56, POCKET MAP G12
Staroměstské náměstí 1.
The **Staré Město Town Hall** occupies a whole sequence of

Kinský Palace, the venue of the fateful speech by Communist prime minister Gottwald

Staré Město Town Hall and Tyn Church on the Old Town Square

houses on Staroměstské náměstí, culminating in an obligatory wedge-tower adorned with a graceful Gothic oriel window. You can check out the historical halls and a handful of rooms that survived World War II, including a pair of former prison cells (charge); it's fun to climb up the tower too (charge). You can also visit the medieval chapel, which has time-worn patches of original wall painting, and wonderful grimacing corbels nestled at the foot of the ribbed vaulting.

If you arrive just before the clock strikes the hour, you'll be able to watch the Apostles marching out on parade.

Astronomical Clock

MAP PAGE 56, POCKET MAP G12
Staroměstské náměstí 1.
By far the most popular sight on Staroměstské náměstí is the town hall's fifteenth-century **Astronomical Clock**, whose hourly mechanical dumbshow (daily, from 9am–9pm) regularly attracts a large crowd of upward-gazing tourists. Little figures of the Apostles shuffle along, bowing to the audience, while perched

on pinnacles below are the four threats to the city as perceived by the medieval mind: Death carrying his hourglass and tolling his bell, Greed with his moneybags, Vanity admiring his reflection, and a turbaned Turk shaking his head. Beneath the figures, four characters representing Philosophy, Religion, Astronomy and History stand motionless throughout the performance. Finally, a cockerel pops out and flaps its wings to signal that the show's over; the clock then chimes the hour and the crowds drift away.

Kinský Palace

MAP PAGE 56, POCKET MAP G11
Staroměstské náměstí 12.
Ⓦ ngprague.cz. Charge.
The largest secular building on Staroměstské náměstí is the Rococo **Kinský Palace**, which is perhaps most notorious as the venue for the fateful speech by the Communist prime minister, **Klement Gottwald**, who walked out onto the grey stone balcony one snowy February morning in 1948, flanked by his Party henchmen, to celebrate the Communist takeover with thousands of supporters

packing the square below. The top two floors house a permanent collection of Asian art, plus temporary exhibitions.

Jan Hus Monument

MAP PAGE 56, POCKET MAP G12
Staroměstské náměstí.

The colossal **Jan Hus Monument** features a turbulent sea of blackened bodies – the oppressed to his right, the defiant to his left – out of which rises the majestic moral authority of Hus himself, a radical religious reformer and martyr from the fifteenth century. On the 500th anniversary of his death, in 1915, the statue was unveiled, but the Austrians refused to hold an official ceremony; in protest, Praguers covered the monument in flowers. Since then, it has been a powerful symbol of Czech nationalism: in March 1939, it was draped in swastikas by the invading Nazis, and in August 1968, it was shrouded in funereal black by Praguers, protesting at the Soviet invasion.

The inscription etched along the base is a quote from the will of pioneering educator John Comenius, one of Hus's seventeenth-century followers. It includes Hus's most famous dictum, *Pravda vitězí* (Truth Prevails), which also appears on the Czech president's official banner.

Church of sv Mikuláš

MAP PAGE 56, POCKET MAP G11–G12
Staroměstské náměstí.

The destruction of the east wing of the town hall in 1945 rudely exposed the Baroque **Church of sv Mikuláš**, built for the Benedictines in 1735. The south front is decidedly luscious, with blackened statuary at every cornice; inside, however, it's a much smaller space, theatrically organized into a series of interlocking curves.

It's also rather plainly furnished, partly because it was closed down by Joseph II and turned into a storehouse, and partly because it's now owned by the very "low", modern, Czechoslovak Hussite Church. Instead, your eyes are drawn sharply upwards to the impressive stuccowork, the wrought-iron galleries and the trompe l'oeil frescoes splashed across the dome.

Jan Hus Monument

Týn church
(Týnský chrám)

MAP PAGE 56, POCKET MAP G12
Celetná 5. ⓦ tyn.cz.

The mighty **Týn church** is by far the most imposing Gothic structure in the Staré Město. Its two irregular towers, bristling with baubles, spires and pinnacles, rise like giant antennae above the arcaded houses which otherwise obscure its facade, and are spectacularly lit up at night. Inside, the church has a lofty, narrow nave punctuated at ground level by black and gold Baroque altarpieces. One or two original Gothic furnishings survive, most notably the pulpit and the fifteenth-century baldachin, housing a winged altar in the north aisle. Behind the pulpit, you'll find another superb winged altar depicting John the Baptist, dating from 1520. The pillar on the right of the chancel steps contains the red marble tomb of **Tycho Brahe**, court astronomer to Rudolf II.

Týn courtyard

MAP PAGE 56, POCKET MAP G11
Hidden behind hulking Týn church is the **Týn courtyard**, also known by its German name, **Ungelt** (meaning "No Money", a pseudonym used to deter marauding invaders), which, as the trading base of German merchants, was one of the first settlements on the Vltava. Later, it was transformed into a palace, only to fall into disrepair during the decades of communist rule. The complex has now come full circle and is once again home to various shops, restaurants and hotels – and the Dominicans, who can often be seen crossing its cobbles.

Church of sv Jakub

MAP PAGE 56, POCKET MAP H11
Malá Štupartská 6.

Before entering this imposingly large church, make sure you admire the distinctive bubbling, stucco portal above the main entrance. The

Church of sv Jakub

church's vast Gothic proportions – it has the longest nave in Prague after the cathedral – make it a favourite venue for organ recitals and other concerts. After the great fire of 1689, Prague's Baroque artists remodelled the interior, adding huge pilasters, a series of colourful frescoes and over twenty side altars.

The **Church of sv Jakub** has close historical links with the butchers of Prague, who are responsible for the thoroughly decomposed and time-shrivelled human forearm you'll see hanging high up on the west wall, on the right as you enter. It has been here for over four hundred years, ever since a thief tried to steal the jewels of the Madonna from the high altar. As the thief reached out, the Virgin supposedly grabbed his arm and refused to let go. The next day, the congregation of butchers had no option but to lop it off, and it has hung there as a warning ever since.

Convent of St Agnes
(Anežský klášter)

MAP PAGE 56, POCKET MAP H10
Anežská 12. ⓦ ngprague.cz. Charge.

Prague's oldest surviving Gothic building, founded in 1233 as a

Franciscan **convent** for the Order of the Poor Clares, now provides a fittingly atmospheric setting for the city's chief **medieval art collection**. The exhibition is arranged chronologically, starting with a remarkable silver-gilt casket from 1360, used to house the skull of St Ludmila. The nine panels from the Vyšší Brod altarpiece, from around 1350, are also among the finest in central Europe. The real gems of the collection, however, are the six panels by Master Theodoric, who produced over one hundred such paintings for Charles IV's castle chapel at Karlštejn. These larger-than-life, half-length portraits of saints, church fathers and so on are full of intense expression and richly coloured detail, their depictions spilling onto the embossed frames. For a glimpse of some extraordinary draughtsmanship, check out the woodcuts by the likes of Cranach the Elder and Dürer – the seven-headed beast in Dürer's *Apocalypse* cycle is particularly Harry Potter. As you exit, you get to see the inside of the Gothic cloisters and the bare church that serves as a resting place for, among others, Václav I (1205–53) and St Agnes herself.

Estates Theatre (Stavovské divadlo)

MAP PAGE 56, POCKET MAP H12
Ovocný trh 1. ⓦ narodni-divadlo.cz/en/stages/the-estates-theatre.

The lime-green and white **Estates Theatre** was built in the early 1780s for the entertainment of Prague's large and powerful German community and remains one of the finest Neoclassical buildings in Prague, reflecting the enormous self-confidence of its patrons. The theatre has a place in Czech history, too, however, for it was here that the **Czech national anthem**, "Kde domov můj?" ("Where is my Home?"), was first performed. It is also a place of pilgrimage for Mozart fans, since it was here that the premieres of *Don Giovanni* and *La Clemenza di Tito* took place – the statue of a hooded figure by the entrance commemorates the fact. This is, in fact, one of the few opera houses in Europe that remains intact from Mozart's time (though it

The fine Neoclassical Estates Theater dates to the 1780s

Church of sv Mikuláš

underwent major refurbishment during the nineteenth century), and it was used by Miloš Forman to film the concert scenes for his Oscar-winning *Amadeus*.

Bethlehem Chapel (Betlémská kaple)

MAP PAGE 56, POCKET MAP F13
Betlémské náměstí 4. Charge.
The often-disregarded **Bethlehem Chapel** was founded in 1391 by religious reformists, who, denied the right to build a church, proceeded instead to build the largest chapel in Bohemia, with a total capacity of exactly 3000 worshippers. Sermons were delivered not in the customary Latin, but in the language of the masses – Czech. From 1402 to 1413, **Jan Hus** famously delivered sermons here, regularly pulling in more than enough commoners to fill the chapel, while the Anabaptist **Thomas Müntzer** also preached here in 1521.

Of the original building, only the three outer walls remain, with restored patches of the biblical scenes which were used to get the message across to the illiterate congregation. The rest is a 1950s reconstruction, made using the original plans and a fair amount of imaginative guesswork. The Communists liked the image of Hus leading the masses against the Church, but he was certainly an odd hero for an atheist regime.

Náprstek Museum

MAP PAGE 56, POCKET MAP H13
Betlémské náměstí 1. ⓦ nm.cz. Charge.
Vojta Náprstek, founder of the **Náprstek Museum**, was inspired by the great Victorian museums of London and turned the family brewery into a museum, initially intending it to concentrate on the virtues of industrial progress. Náprstek's interests gradually shifted towards anthropology, however, and it is his ethnographic collections from the Americas, Australasia and Oceania that are now on display. Despite the fact that the museum could clearly do with an injection of cash, it still manages to put on some really excellent temporary ethnographic exhibitions on the ground floor, and also does a useful job of promoting tolerance of different cultures.

Shops

Antik v Dlouhé

MAP PAGE 56, POCKET MAP H11
Dlouhá 37. Ⓦ antik-v-dlouhe.cz.
Great antique shop with many
authentic items that will fit in a
suitcase, though it does specialize in
spectacular light fittings and First
Republic chrome tube chairs.

Art Deco

MAP PAGE 56, POCKET MAP G12
Michalská 21. Ⓦ artdecogalerie.cz.
A stylish antiques trove overflowing
with clothes, hats, teapots, glasses,
clocks and twentieth-century art.

Botanicus

MAP PAGE 56, POCKET MAP H11
Týn 3. Ⓦ botanicus.cz.
Czech take on the UK's Body Shop,
with a more folksy ambience. Dried
flowers, handmade paper and fancy
honey are sold alongside natural
soaps and shampoos.

Botas 66

MAP PAGE 56, POCKET MAP G13
Skořepka 4. Ⓦ bteam.cz.

The products of this communist-era
sneaker company have been brought
back from the dead, reproduced in
garish hues and sold as "retro".

Bric a Brac

MAP PAGE 56, POCKET MAP G11
Týnská 7. Ⓦ prague-antique-shop.com.
Absolutely minute antiques store,
packed to the rafters with trinkets.
The central location means that
prices are quite high, but it's worth
visiting for the spectacle alone.
The owner also runs a larger place
round the corner.

Disko Duck

MAP PAGE 56, POCKET MAP F12
Karlova 12. Ⓦ diskoduck.cz.
With some five thousand records
in stock, ranging from house, hip
hop, r'n'b and techno to electro,
jungle and breakbeat, *Disko Duck*
is bound to have something in
stock that you didn't even know
that you needed.

Gábina Páralová

MAP PAGE 56, POCKET MAP H11
Jakubská 14. Ⓦ gabinaparalova.cz.
Home-grown designer Gábina
Páralová creates casual outfits with

Kubista, a lifestyle store in a beautiful Cubist building

surprising details and lively twists. Her independent shop is a good place to get a fresh look at the Czech fashion scene.

Granát turnov

MAP PAGE 56, POCKET MAP H11
Celetná dlouhá 28. Ⓦ granat.cz/en/company-stores/prague-dlouha-str.
The best place to get your mitts on some exquisite Bohemian garnet jewellery, made in North Bohemia.

Havelská Market

MAP PAGE 56, POCKET MAP G12
Havelská 13. Mon–Sat 7am–7pm, Sun 8am–6.30pm.
Open-air market stretching the full length of the arcaded street of Havelská, selling fruit, flowers, vegetables, CDs, souvenirs, wooden toys and more.

Hračky u zlatého lva

MAP PAGE 56, POCKET MAP H12
Celetná 32. Ⓦ eshop.ceskehracky.com.
A huge multistorey toy shop specializing in wooden items, many featuring a *Krtek* (Little Mole – the most popular Czech cartoon character) theme.

Kavka

MAP PAGE 56, POCKET MAP F13
Krocínova 5. Ⓦ kavkabook.cz.
Aptly housed in a thoroughbred functionalist building, this superb store is crammed with every conceivable book on the subject of Czech art and photography.

Kubista

MAP PAGE 56, POCKET MAP H12
Ovocný trh 19. Ⓦ kubista.cz.
Beautiful shop housed in Prague's most impressively preserved Cubist building, selling reproductions of exquisite Cubist ceramics, jewellery and furniture.

Manufaktura

MAP PAGE 56, POCKET MAP G12
Melantrichova 17. Ⓦ manufaktura.cz.
Czech folk-inspired shop with an array of traditional wooden

Fresh fruits at the Havelská Market

toys, painted Easter eggs, straw decorations, honeycomb candles and kitchen utensils.

Monarch

MAP PAGE 56, POCKET MAP G13
Na Perštýně 15. Ⓦ monarch.cz.
Arguably the city's number one wine shop (and wine bar), with stock from all over the world as well as local produce – it sells cheese and dried meats, too.

Prague Fashion Museum

MAP PAGE 56, POCKET MAP H12
Štupartská 3. ☏ 608 227 561.
Miniscule shop showcasing seven decades of fantastic vintage finds, with stock ranging from rare clothing and designer shoes to accessories and jewellery.

Sparta Praha

MAP PAGE 56, POCKET MAP G13
Betlémské náměstí 7. ☏ 608 231 167.
Centrally located football-fan shop stocking everything from soccer shirts to ashtrays, mostly for Sparta Praha, but additionally Slavia Praha, Bohemians and Dukla Praha merchandise.

Cafés

Au Gourmand

MAP PAGE 56, POCKET MAP G11
Dlouhá 10. Ⓦ augourmand.cz.
Beautifully tiled French boulangerie, patisserie and *traiteur* selling wickedly delicious pastries. Kč

Bakeshop Praha

MAP PAGE 56, POCKET MAP G11
Kozí 1. Ⓦ bakeshop.cz.
Three days into a trip to central Europe and already pining for a cupcake or small bucket of coffee? Then head to this expat bakery in the very heart of the Old Town. Kč

Beas Vegetarian Dhaba

MAP PAGE 56, POCKET MAP H11
Týnská 19. Ⓦ dhababeas.cz.
Bright, modern Indian veggie café through the courtyard off Týnská, offering authentic dosas and thalis served on basic metal trays. Kč

Café No.3

MAP PAGE 56, POCKET MAP H11
Jakubská 3. ☎ 602 255 918.
Cosy hangout with a good selection of coffees and teas (and great hot

Hračky u zlatého lva toy store

chocolate, too). Also serves up filling sandwiches and cakes, but the dish to go for here is the stack of pancakes. Kč

Cathedral Café

MAP PAGE 56, POCKET MAP H11
Týnská 1. Ⓦ cathedralcafe.cz.
Romantic little haunt opening out onto a lush green courtyard, serving fantastic coffee and a brunch menu with all the classics cooked extremely well (think pancakes, smoked salmon bagels and eggs benedict).

Country Life

MAP PAGE 56, POCKET MAP G12
Melantrichova 15. Ⓦ countrylife.cz/
prodejna-country-life-melantrichova.
Self-service vegan café behind the health food shop of the same name: pile up your plate with hot or cold dishes and salad and pay by weight. Kč

Crème de la Crème

MAP PAGE 56, POCKET MAP G12
Husova 12. Ⓦ cremedelacreme.cz.
Multinational *gelateria* that serves up some of the best ice cream in Prague, containing delicious real fruit and nothing it shouldn't. Kč

Grand Café Orient

MAP PAGE 56, POCKET MAP H12
Ovocný trh 19. Ⓦ grandcafeorient.cz.
This superb reconstruction of a famous Cubist café from 1911 dishes up freshly baked cakes, pancakes and excellent coffee, and there's a lovely narrow balcony for sunny days. Kč

Havelská koruna

MAP PAGE 56, POCKET MAP G12
Havelská 21. Ⓦ havelska-koruna.com.
Popular, no-frills *jídelna* (self-service canteen), with utilitarian bench seating and a countryside-style menu of comfort food with the Czechs' favourite side dish – dumplings. So many foreigners wind up here that staff speak some English. Kč

Montmartre

MAP PAGE 56, POCKET MAP F12
Řetězová 7. ☏ 601 364 137.

Classic, small, barrel-vaulted café, the "Montík" was once a famous First Republic dance and cabaret venue, frequented by the likes of Werfel, Jesenská and Hašek. Nowadays, it's a lot quieter, attracting a good mix of students and locals. Kč

Restaurants

Gruzie Restaurant

MAP PAGE 56, POCKET MAP G11
Bílkova 861/14. ⓦ gruzierestaurant.cz.

Atmospheric and cavernous Georgian restaurant serving a menu of classic dishes from the Caucasus, including meat dumplings and grilled meat cooked to order over a charcoal grill. Be sure to order a side of cheese-topped bread. KčKčKč

Lehká hlava (Clear Head)

MAP PAGE 56, POCKET MAP F13
Boršov 2. ⓦ lehkahlava.cz.

Exotic, cave-like veggie restaurant located just off Karoliny světlé, serving eclectic international mains such as no-beef steaks with dumplings, bun-cha with vegan pork belly, and burritos. KčKč

Lokál

MAP PAGE 56, POCKET MAP H11
Dlouhá 33. ⓦ lokal-dlouha.ambi.cz.

Vast corridor of a restaurant, decked out in sleek decor. Waiters in long white aprons serve up excellent Czech pub food. KčKč

Naše maso

MAP PAGE 56, POCKET MAP H11
Dlouhá 39. ⓦ nasemaso.cz.

Part of the 1930s Gurmet Pasáž Dlouhá complex, this madly popular, hipster-style butchery has just six (much-coveted) seats. Expect long queues at mealtimes for the superb salamis, meatloaf, hamburgers and sausages. KčKč

Grand Café Orient

Maitrea

MAP PAGE 56, POCKET MAP G11
Týnská ulička 6. ⓦ restaurace-maitrea.cz.

This larger, more luxurious branch of *Lehká hlava* is a den of stylish Buddhist calm, serving global vegetarian dishes. KčKčKč

Mincovna

MAP PAGE 56, POCKET MAP G11
Staroměstské náměstí 7.
ⓦ restauracemincovna.cz.

If you must do your dining on the Old Town Square, head for *Mincovna*. This is the least touristy, most reasonably priced and most understatedly Czech restaurant there. Mains include traditional beef shoulder with dumplings and cream sauce or vegetarian options like cauliflower pancakes. KčKčKč

Mlýnec

MAP PAGE 56, POCKET MAP F12
Novotného lávka 9. ⓦ mlynec.cz.

A pricey place (which has occasionally garnered Michelin stars) with a fabulous riverside terrace overlooking Charles Bridge. The menu covers Czech staples, such as traditional duck leg confit, and Asian fusion dishes. There's also a popular brunch menu which includes a starter, main, dessert and a glass of prosecco. KčKčKčKč

Rybárna

MAP PAGE 56, POCKET MAP G11
Masná 1. ⓦ rybarna.net.

This great fishmonger-café claims to serve the freshest seafood in town, offering a guarantee that your order was swimming or crawling in the North Sea or Mediterranean under 24 hours before it arrived on your plate. Choose your critter and have it cooked as you like. KčKčKčKč

Stoleti

MAP PAGE 56, POCKET MAP F13
Karoliny Světlé 21. ⓦ stoleti.cz.

Imaginative Czech cuisine named after stars of film and stage, all served in an unstuffy and simply furnished restaurant. KčKčKč

U provaznice

MAP PAGE 56, POCKET MAP H13
Provaznická 3. ⓦ uprovaznice.cz.

Hidden down a backstreet behind Můstek metro station, this tiled and timbered, tourist-free Czech pub-restaurant plates up no-nonsense Czech favourites at time-warped prices. KčKč

Pubs and bars

Blatnička

MAP PAGE 56, POCKET MAP G12
Michalská 5. ☏ 224 225 860.

Long-established wine shop where you can drink straight from the barrel, take away, or head next door to the popular basement *vinárna* for more wine and inexpensive snacks.

James Joyce

MAP PAGE 56, POCKET MAP G10
U Obecního dvora 4. ⓦ jamesjoyceprague.cz.

The best of Prague's Irish pubs, with real Irish staff, an open fire, draught Kilkenny and Guinness and decent Irish-themed food.

Kozička

MAP PAGE 56, POCKET MAP G11
Kozí 4. ⓦ kozicka.cz.

Busy, designer, bare-brick cellar bar with cheap Czech food, tucked away just a short walk from bustling Staroměstské náměstí.

Prague Beer Museum

MAP PAGE 56, POCKET MAP H11
Dlouhá 46. ⓦ praguebeermuseum.cz.

For some authentic Czech beer, head to this characterful drinking

National Marionette Theatre

den with thirty types on draught,
including pilsners, dark lagers,
wheat beers, IPAs and more, from
across the country.

U medvídků
(The Little Bears)

MAP PAGE 56, POCKET MAP G13
Na Perštýně 7. Ⓦ umedvidku.cz.
A popular Prague beer hall dating
back to the thirteenth century
– and still much the same as it
always has been (make sure you
turn right when you enter, and
avoid the bar to the left). The
Budvar flows freely, and the food is
reliably Bohemian.

U rudolfina

MAP PAGE 56, POCKET MAP F11
Křížovnická 10. Ⓦ urudolfina.cz.
A proper Czech *pivnice* serving
beautifully kept Pilsner Urquell
and typical pub grub, very close to
Charles Bridge.

U zlatého tygra
(The Golden Tiger)

MAP PAGE 56, POCKET MAP F12
Husova 17. Ⓦ uzlatehotygra.cz.
Small central *pivnice*, always busy
with locals and tourists trying
to nab a seat; the late writer and
Bohemian, Bohumil Hrabal, was a
semi-permanent resident.

Clubs and venues

AghaRTA Jazz Centrum

MAP PAGE 56, POCKET MAP G12
Železná 16. Ⓦ agharta.cz.
An excellent central jazz club,
with a combination of Czech and
foreign patrons, a consistently
good programme of gigs and a
round-the-year festival that brings
in some top acts.

Chapeau Rouge

MAP PAGE 56, POCKET MAP H11
Jakubská 2. Ⓦ chapeaurouge.cz.
Centrally located, multi-floor,
good-time club, with a blood-
red bar on the ground floor (free

AghaRTA Jazz Centrum

entry) and two dancefloors above
featuring either DJs or live bands.

Estates Theatre
(Stavovské divadlo)

MAP PAGE 56, POCKET MAP H12
Ovocný trh 1. Ⓦ narodni-divadlo.cz.
Known for its Mozart connections,
Prague's oldest opera house has
a glorious nineteenth-century
interior and puts on a mixture
of theatre, ballet and opera (with
English subtitles). Guided building
tours are available outside of
performance times.

National
Marionette Theatre

MAP PAGE 56, POCKET MAP F11
Žatecká 1. ☎ 224 819 322.
It could be corny but this is
actually good fun – Mozart's operas
performed by giant marionettes.
There's an early kids' show of *The
Magic Flute*.

Roxy

MAP PAGE 56, POCKET MAP H11
Dlouhá 33. Ⓦ roxy.cz.
Roxy is a great little venue: a
laidback, rambling old theatre with
a programme ranging from arty
films and exhibitions to top live
acts and DJ nights.

Josefov

The old Jewish ghetto district of Josefov remains one of the most remarkable sights in Prague and an essential slice of the city's cultural heritage. Although the warren-like street plan of the old ghetto was demolished in the 1890s – to make way for avenues of luxurious five-storey mansions – six synagogues, the Jewish Town Hall and the medieval cemetery still survive. They were preserved under the Nazis as a record of communities they had destroyed. To this end, Jewish artefacts from Czechoslovakia and beyond were gathered here and, today, make up one of the most comprehensive collections of Judaica in Europe.

Památník jaroslava ježka

MAP PAGE 72, POCKET MAP G11
Kaprova 10. Ⓦ nm.cz. Charge.
If you happen to be in the Josefov area on a Tuesday afternoon, it's worth taking the opportunity to visit the **Památník Jaroslava**

Ježka, which occupies one room of the first-floor flat of the avant-garde composer Jaroslav Ježek (1906–42), at Kaprova 10. It's a great way to escape the crowds, hear some of Ježek's music, and admire the Modrý pokoj (Blue

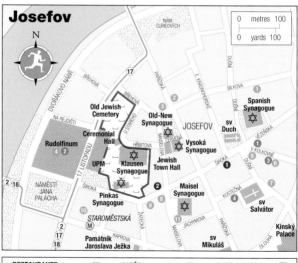

RESTAURANTS		CAFÉS		PUBS & BARS	
Dinitz	1	Mezi řádky	10	Kenton's New	
James Dean	6	Nostress	5	York Bar	3
King Solomon	11	Rudolfinum	4	Krčma	4
Kolonial	8			V kolkovně	1
La Veranda	2	SHOPS			
Les Moules	3	Judaica	2	VENUE	
Praha MATZIP	7	La Bretagne	1	Rudolfinum	2
U golema	9				

Room), with its functionalist furniture and grand piano, in which he did his composing.

Náměstí Jana Palacha

MAP PAGE 72, POCKET MAP F11

On the Josefov riverfront is **Náměstí Jana Palacha**, previously known as Red Army Square and embellished with a flowerbed in the shape of a red star (now replaced by an anonymous circular vent), in memory of the Soviet dead who were temporarily buried here in May 1945. The building on the east side of the square is the Faculty of Philosophy, where Jan Palach (see page 108) was a student (his bust adorns a corner of the building).

Old-New Synagogue (Staronová synagoga)

MAP PAGE 72, POCKET MAP G11
Červená 2. Charge.

The **Old-New Synagogue** (Staronová synagoga or Altneuschul) got its hybrid name from the fact that when it was built it was indeed very new, though eventually it became the oldest synagogue in Josefov. Begun in the second half of the thirteenth century, and featuring a wonderful set of steep, sawtooth brick gables, it is, in fact, the oldest functioning synagogue in Europe, one of the earliest Gothic buildings in Prague and still the religious centre for Prague's Orthodox Jews. To get to the **main hall**, you must pass through one of the two low vestibules from which women watch the proceedings through narrow slits. Above the entrance is an elaborate tympanum covered

Staronová synagoga

in the twisting branches of a vine tree, its twelve bunches of grapes representing the tribes of Israel. The simple, plain interior is mostly taken up with the elaborate wrought-iron cage enclosing the bimah in the centre. The tattered red standard on display was originally a gift to the community from Emperor Ferdinand II for helping fend off the Swedes in 1648.

Jewish Town Hall (Židovská radnice)

MAP PAGE 72, POCKET MAP G11
Maiselova 18. Not open to the public.

The **Jewish Town Hall** is one of the few such buildings in central Europe to survive the Holocaust. Founded and funded by Mordecai Maisel, minister of finance to Rudolf II, in the sixteenth century, it was later rebuilt as the creamy-pink Baroque

Visiting Josefov's sights

All the major sights of Josefov – the Old-New Synagogue, Old Jewish Cemetery, the Ceremonial Hall, the Maisel, Pinkas, Klausen and Spanish synagogues – are part of the **Jewish Museum** (ⓦjewishmuseum.cz) and covered by an **all-in-one ticket**, available from any of the quarter's numerous **ticket offices** (main office at U staré školy 1).

The neo-Gothic Maisel Synagogue

house you now see. The belfry has a clock on each of its four sides, plus a Hebrew one, stuck on the north gable, which, like the Hebrew script, goes "backwards".

Maisel Synagogue (Maiselova synagoga)

MAP PAGE 72, POCKET MAP G11
Maiselova 10.

Like the town hall, the neo-Gothic **Maisel Synagogue** was founded and paid for entirely by Mordecai Maisel. Set back from the neighbouring houses south down Maiselova, the synagogue was, in its day, one of the most ornate in Josefov. Nowadays, its bare, whitewashed interior houses an exhibition on the history of the Czech–Jewish community up until the 1781 Edict of Tolerance. Along with glass cabinets filled with gold and silverwork, Hanukkah candlesticks, Torah scrolls and other religious artefacts, there's also an example of the antiquated ruffs that had to be worn by all unmarried males from the age of twelve, and a copy of Ferdinand I's decree enforcing the wearing of a circular yellow badge.

Klub za starou Prahu

Around 600 houses were demolished in the great Josefov *asanace*, the biggest incursion into the medieval fabric of the Czech capital ever to be permitted by the city authorities. The same fate awaited the Old Town and Malá Strana, the overzealous planners looking to transform medieval Prague into a kind of *fin de siècle* Paris on the Vltava. However, even in the late nineteenth century many Prague dwellers could see the value of their city's heritage and launched a campaign to stop the destruction. This led to the creation of one of Prague's most important civic movements – the **Klub za starou Prahu** (Old Prague Club, ⦿ zastarouprahu. cz), which to this day continues to highlight the excesses of unscrupulous developers and call out corrupt city councillors whose actions threaten the integrity of this most precious city.

Pinkas Synagogue (Pinkasov synagoga)

MAP PAGE 72, POCKET MAP F11
Široká 3.

Built in the 1530s for the powerful Horovitz family, the **Pinkas Synagogue** has undergone countless restorations over the centuries. In 1958, the synagogue was transformed into a chilling memorial to the 77,297 Czech Jews killed during the Holocaust. The memorial was closed shortly after the 1967 Six Day War – due to damp, according to the Communists – and remained so, allegedly due to problems with the masonry, until it was finally, painstakingly restored in the 1990s. All that remains of the synagogue's original decor today is the ornate bimah surrounded by a beautiful wrought-iron grille, supported by barley-sugar columns.

Of all the sights of the Jewish quarter, the **Holocaust memorial** is perhaps the most moving, with every bit of wall space taken up with the carved stone list of victims, stating simply their name, date of birth and date of death or transportation to the camps. It is the longest epitaph in the world, yet it represents a mere fraction of those who died in the Nazi concentration camps. Upstairs in a room beside the women's gallery, there's also a harrowing exhibition of drawings by children from the Jewish ghetto in Terezín, most of whom were killed in the camps.

Old Jewish Cemetery (Starý židovský hřbitov)

MAP PAGE 72, POCKET MAP F11
Široká 3.

At the heart of Josefov is the **Old Jewish Cemetery**, which you enter from the Pinkas Synagogue and leave by the Klausen Synagogue. Established in the fifteenth century, it was in use until 1787, by which time there were an estimated 100,000 people buried here, one on top of the other, six palms

apart, and as many as twelve layers deep. The enormous number of visitors has meant that the graves themselves have been roped off to protect them, but if you get there before the crowds – a difficult task for much of the year – the cemetery can be a poignant reminder of the ghetto, its inhabitants subjected to inhuman overcrowding even in death. The rest of Prague recedes beyond the tall ash trees and cramped perimeter walls, the haphazard headstones and Hebrew inscriptions casting a powerful spell. On many graves, you'll see pebbles, some holding down *kvitlech* or small messages of supplication.

Ceremonial Hall (Obřadní sín)

MAP PAGE 72, POCKET MAP F11
U starého hřbitova.

Immediately on your left as you leave the cemetery is the **Ceremonial Hall**, a lugubrious neo-Renaissance house built in 1906 as a ceremonial hall by the Jewish Burial Society. Appropriately enough, it's now devoted to an exhibition on Jewish traditions of burial and death, though it would probably be more useful if you

Klausen Synagogue

could visit it before heading into the cemetery, rather than after.

Klausen Synagogue (Klausova synagoga)

MAP PAGE 72, POCKET MAP F11
U starého hřbitova 1.

A late seventeenth-century building, the **Klausen Synagogue** was founded in the 1690s by Mordecai Maisel on the site of several small buildings (Klausen), in what was then a notorious red-light district of Josefov. The ornate Baroque interior contains a rich display of religious objects from embroidered *kippah* to Kiddush cups, and explains the very basics of Jewish religious practice, and the chief festivals or High Holidays.

Pařížská

MAP PAGE 72, POCKET MAP F10–G11
Running through the heart of the old ghetto is **Pařížská**, the ultimate bourgeois avenue, lined with buildings covered in a riot of late nineteenth-century sculpturing, spikes and turrets. At odds with the rest of Josefov, its ground-floor premises are home to designer label clothes and accessory shops, jewellery stores and swanky cafés, restaurants and bars.

Old Jewish Cemetery

Rudolfinum

MAP PAGE 72, POCKET MAP F11
Alšovo nábřeží 12. ⓦ rudolfinum.cz.

The **Rudolfinum**, or House of Artists (Dům umělců), is one of the proud civic buildings of the nineteenth-century Czech national revival. Built to house an art gallery, museum and concert hall for the Czech-speaking community, it became the seat of the new Czechoslovak parliament from 1919 until 1941 when it was closed down by the Nazis. Since 1946, the building has returned to its original artistic purpose and it's now one of the capital's main concert venues (home to the Czech Philharmonic) and exhibition spaces.

UPM (Museum of Decorative Arts)

MAP PAGE 72, POCKET MAP F11
17 listopadu 2. ⓦ upm.cz.

From its foundation in 1885 through to the end of the First Republic, the **Uměleckoprůmyslové muzeum** or **UPM** received the best that the Czech modern movement had to offer – from Art Nouveau to the avant-garde – and its collection is consequently unrivalled. The building itself is richly decorated in mosaics, stained glass and sculptures, and its ground-floor temporary exhibitions are consistently excellent.

In recent years, the UPM has undergone a complete rebuild, which has meant the exhibitions have been closed while work is completed. The aim was to more clearly define the curation of its collections after its 2018 re-opening. These include textiles and richly embroidered religious vestments from the fifteenth to the eighteenth centuries, lacework from down the ages, costumes spanning three centuries, and impressive glass, ceramic and pottery displays – for many the highlight of the entire UPM. They also cover furniture, jewellery, curios, Czech photography, interwar prints, works by Josef Sudek, avant-garde graphics by Karel Teige, book designs by Josef Váchal and some of Alfons Mucha's famous turn-of-the-twentieth-century Parisian advertising posters.

Spanish Synagogue (Španělská synagoga)

MAP PAGE 72, POCKET MAP G11

Vězeňská 1.

Built in 1868, the **Spanish Synagogue** is by far the most ornate synagogue in Josefov, its stunning, gilded Moorish interior deliberately imitating the Alhambra (hence its name). Every available surface is drowning in a profusion of floral motifs and geometric patterns, in vibrant reds, greens and blues, which are repeated in the synagogue's huge stained-glass windows. The synagogue now houses an interesting exhibition on the history of Prague's Jews from the time of the 1781 Edict of Tolerance to the Holocaust. Lovely, slender, painted cast-iron columns hold up the women's gallery, where the displays include a fascinating set of photos depicting the old ghetto at the time of its demolition. There's a

The Moorish-style Spanish Synagogue

section on Prague's German–Jewish writers, including Kafka, and information on the Holocaust. In the upper-floor prayer hall, there's an exhibition of silver religious artefacts – a mere fraction of the six thousand pieces collected here, initially for Prague's Jewish Museum (founded in 1906), with more gathered later under the Nazis.

The Golem

Legends concerning the animation of unformed matter (which is what the Hebrew word **golem** means), using the mystical texts of the Kabbala, were around long before Frankenstein started playing around with corpses. The most famous golem was the giant servant made from the mud of the Vltava by **Rabbi Löw**, the sixteenth-century chief rabbi of Prague. It was brought to life when the rabbi placed a *shem*, a tablet with a magic Hebrew inscription, in its mouth.

There are numerous versions of the tale, though none earlier than the nineteenth century. In some, the golem is a figure of fun, flooding the rabbi's kitchen rather in the manner of Disney's *Sorcerer's Apprentice*; others portray him as the guardian of the ghetto, helping Rabbi Löw in his struggle with the anti-Semites at the court of Rudolf II. In almost all versions, however, the golem finally runs amok and Löw has to remove the *shem* once and for all, and hide the creature away in the attic of the Old-New Synagogue (see page 73), where it has supposedly resided ever since – ready to come out again if needed.

Shops

Judaica

MAP PAGE 72, POCKET MAP F11
Široká 7.
Probably the best-stocked of all
the places selling Jewish titles to
tourists, with books and prints,
secondhand and new.

La Bretagne

MAP PAGE 72, POCKET MAP G11
Široká 22.
There's a wide array of fresh fish
and seafood at this centrally located
fishmonger's, plus takeaway sushi.

Cafés

Mezi řádky

MAP PAGE 72, POCKET MAP F11
Palachovo náměstí 2.
ⓦ etincelle.cz/kavarny-a-bistra.
Join Charles University's students
and professors at this no-frills café
deep within the humanities faculty
building. Cheap Czech staples –
meatloaf, salads drowning in mayo,
open sandwiches – plus beer and

wine. To find it, enter the building
and turn immediately right. Kč

Nostress

MAP PAGE 72, POCKET MAP G11
Dušní 10. ⓦ nostress.cz.
Colourful café with lots of bright
cushions and indoor trees. Claims
to have served Prague's best
coffee for two decades – stress-
test this alternative fact between
synagogues. Kč

Rudolfinum

MAP PAGE 72, POCKET MAP F11
Alšovo nábřeží 12. ⓦ rudolfinum.cz.
Splendidly grand nineteenth-
century café on the first floor of the
Rudolfinum, serving drinks and
snacks amid potted palms. Worth
seeing, even if you're not thirsty. Kč

Restaurants

Dinitz

MAP PAGE 72, POCKET MAP G11
Bílková 12. ⓦ dinitz.cz.
Kosher restaurant with Middle
Eastern snacks, sandwiches, pasta,
salads and mains. KčKč

James Dean

MAP PAGE 72, POCKET MAP G11
V Kolkovně 1. ⓦ jamesdean.cz.
This retro American diner has an
authentic-looking interior, ceiling
fans, a twangy soundtrack and staff
dressed for the part. Go hungry;
portions of burgers and fries are
Cadillac size. Kč

King Solomon

MAP PAGE 72, POCKET MAP F11
Široká 8. ⓦ kosher.cz.
Sophisticated kosher restaurant
serving big helpings of
international dishes and traditional
Jewish specialities. KčKčKčKč

Kolonial

MAP PAGE 72, POCKET MAP F11
Široká 6. ① 224 818 322.
The first things you'll notice
are the penny-farthings in the

Belgian brasserie Les Moules

window, and the old enamel bicycle adverts and saddle bar stools continue the cycling theme inside. The menu is a mixed pannier, ranging from roast pork knee to Caesar salad. KčKč

La Veranda

MAP PAGE 72, POCKET MAP G11
Elišky Krásnohorské 10. ⓦ laveranda.cz.
Family-run restaurant focused on local ingredients and fresh cooking, with wonderful staff who really add to the experience – take their recommendations when ordering. Mains range from lamb shoulder in brown butter to grilled pikeperch. KčKčKč

Les Moules

MAP PAGE 72, POCKET MAP G11
Pařížská 19. ⓦ lesmoules.cz.
One of a chain of wood-panelled Belgian brasseries which flies in fresh mussels, pairing them with French fries and Belgian beers. KčKčKč

Praha MATZIP

MAP PAGE 72, POCKET MAP G11
Dušní 1082/6. ⓦ prahamatzip.com.
Expect authentic kimchi pancakes, freshly prepared *bibimbap* and plenty of enticing Korean classics at this cosy hidden gem. KčKč

U Golema

MAP PAGE 72, POCKET MAP G11
Maiselova 8. ⓣ 222 328 165.
Golem himself greets diners at this pleasant restaurant in Josefov's sightseeing zone. The hearty, meat-themed menu consists mainly of Czech food, with a few French influences. KčKčKč

Pubs and bars

Kenton's New York Bar

MAP PAGE 72, POCKET MAP G11
V kolkovně 3. ⓦ kentons.cz.
Sophisticated and smart American cocktail bar, with professional staff and a great atmosphere.

La Veranda

Krčma

MAP PAGE 72, POCKET MAP G11
Kostečná 4. ⓦ krcma.cz.
If you don't fancy riding the wave of gentrification around Pařížská, seek out this cellar tavern for some candlelit, faux-medieval Czech grit. The Urquell is cheap, and the old-Bohemian food realistically priced.

V kolkovně

MAP PAGE 72, POCKET MAP G11
V kolkovně 8. ⓦ kolkovna.cz/cs/kolkovna-v-kolkovne-26.
Justifiably popular with passing tourists, this Pilsner Urquell drinking den has plush decor, excellent pub food and unpasteurized Pilsner on tap.

Venue

Rudolfinum

MAP PAGE 72, POCKET MAP F11
Alšovo nábřeží 12. ⓦ rudolfinum.cz.
A stunning neo-Renaissance concert hall from the late nineteenth century that's home to the Czech Philharmonic.

Wenceslas Square and northern Nové Město

Nové Město – Prague's "New Town" – is the city's main commercial and business district, housing most of its big hotels, cinemas, nightclubs, fast-food outlets and department stores. Architecturally, it comes over as big, bourgeois and predominantly fin de siècle, yet the large market squares and wide streets were actually laid out way back in the fourteenth century by Emperor Charles IV. The obvious starting point in Nové Město is Wenceslas Square (Václavské náměstí), the long, sloping boulevard with its distinctive, interwar shopping malls, which is where Czechs traditionally gather when they have something to protest about and is today at the hub of the modern city.

Wenceslas Square (Václavské náměstí)

MAP PAGE 82, POCKET MAP H13–J13

The natural pivot around which modern Prague revolves, **Wenceslas Square** is more of a wide, gently sloping boulevard than a traditional square as such. It's scarcely a conventional – or even convenient – space in which

David Černý's sculpture in Lucerna pasáž

to hold mass demonstrations, yet for the past 150 years or more it has been the focus of political protest in Prague. In August 1968, it was the scene of some of the most violent confrontations between the Soviet invaders and the local Czechs. More happily, in late November 1989, more than 250,000 people crammed into the square night after night, often enduring sub-zero temperatures, to demand free elections.

Despite the square's history and its medieval origins, it is now a thoroughly modern, glitzy, slightly seedy boulevard, lined with self-important six- or seven-storey buildings representing every artistic and architectural trend of the past hundred years, from neo-Renaissance to Socialist Realism. At the top of the square, in front of the grandiose National Museum, stands the **Wenceslas Monument**, a worthy and heroic, but pretty unexciting, equestrian statue of the country's patron saint. Beneath the statue, a simple memorial commemorating the victims of Communism is adorned with flowers and photos of Jan Palach

Wenceslas Square, the core of modern Prague

and Jan Zajíc, both of whom martyred themselves here in 1969 in protest at the Soviet invasion.

Lucerna pasáž

MAP PAGE 82, POCKET MAP H14

Wenceslas Square has an impressive array of old shopping arcades, or *pasáže*, as they're known in Czech, mostly dating from the interwar period. The king of the lot is the lavishly decorated fin-de-siècle **Lucerna pasáž**, stretching all the way from Štěpánská to Vodičkova. Designed in the early part of the twentieth century in Moorish style by, among others, Václav Havel's own grandfather, it boasts an ornate cinema, café and vast concert hall. Suspended from the ceiling in the centre of the arcade is David Černý's parody of the square's equestrian Wenceslas Monument, with the saint astride an upside-down charger.

National Museum (Národní muzeum)

MAP PAGE 82, POCKET MAP J14

Václavské náměstí 68. Ⓦ nm.cz. Charge.
Built in 1890, the broad, brooding hulk of the **National Museum** dominates the view up Wenceslas

Square like a giant golden eagle with outstretched wings. When it finally reopens after drawn-out and much-delayed renovation work, museum chiefs promise a focus on interactive natural history displays. Be sure to admire the ornate marble entrance hall and splendid monumental staircase leading to the glass-domed Pantheon, with its 48 busts and statues of bewhiskered Czech men (plus a couple of token women and Slovaks). Those with a cultural itch might head next door to the **New Building** (Vinohradská 1; charge), with exhibitions ranging from Czech archeology to scientific and cultural milestones.

Prague Main Train Station (Praha hlavní nádraží)

MAP PAGE 82, POCKET MAP K13

Prague Main Train Station is one of the final architectural glories of the dying Habsburg Empire, designed by **Josef Fanta** and officially opened in 1909 as the Franz-Josefs Bahnhof. Arriving by metro, or buying tickets in the over-polished subterranean modern section, it's easy to miss the station's recently renovated Art Nouveau

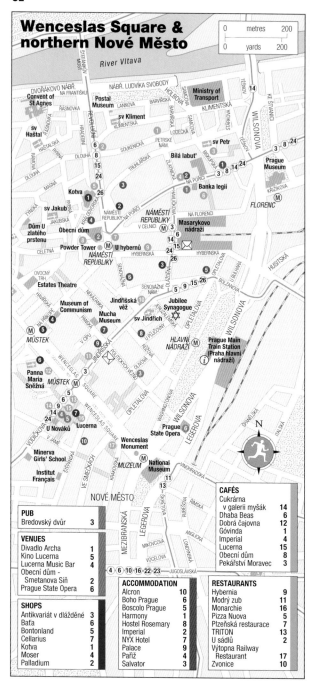

Wenceslas Square & northern Nové Město

| 0 | metres | 200 |
| 0 | yards | 200 |

PUB

| Bredovský dvůr | 3 |

VENUES

Divadlo Archa	1
Kino Lucerna	5
Lucerna Music Bar	4
Obecní dům – Smetanova Síň	2
Prague State Opera	6

SHOPS

Antikvariát v dlážděné	3
Baťa	6
Bontonland	5
Cellarius	7
Kotva	1
Moser	4
Palladium	2

ACCOMMODATION

Alcron	10
Boho Prague	6
Boscolo Prague	5
Harmony	1
Hostel Rosemary	8
Imperial	2
NYX Hotel	7
Palace	9
Paříž	4
Salvator	3

CAFÉS

Cukrárna v galerii myšák	14
Dhaba Beas	6
Dobrá čajovna	12
Góvinda	1
Imperial	4
Lucerna	15
Obecní dům	8
Pekářství Moravec	3

RESTAURANTS

Hybernia	9
Modrý zub	11
Monarchie	16
Pizza Nuova	5
Plzeňská restaurace	7
TRITON	13
U sádlů	2
Výtopna Railway Restaurant	17
Zvonice	10

parts. Upstairs, the original entrance – now blighted by a motorway outside – still exudes imperial confidence, with its wrought-iron canopy and naked figurines clinging to the sides of the towers.

Jubilee Synagogue

MAP PAGE 82, POCKET MAP J12
Jeruzalémská. Charge.

Named in honour of the sixtieth year of the Emperor Franz-Josef I's reign in 1908, the **Jubilee Synagogue** was built in an incredibly colourful Moorish style similar to that of the Spanish Synagogue in Josefov, but with a touch of Art Nouveau. The Hebrew quote from Malachi on the facade strikes a note of liberal optimism: "Do we not have one father? Were we not created by the same God?"

Jindříšská věž

MAP PAGE 82, POCKET MAP J12

This freestanding fifteenth-century tower is the belfry of the nearby church of **sv Jindřich** (St Henry), whose digitally controlled, high-pitched bells ring out every fifteen minutes, and play an entire medley every four hours. In contrast to every other surviving tower in Prague, the **Jindříšská věž** has been imaginatively and expensively restored and now contains a café, restaurant, shop, exhibition space and, on the top floor, a small **museum** (charge) on Prague's hundred-plus towers, with a good view across the city's rooftops.

Mucha Museum

MAP PAGE 82, POCKET MAP H12–H13
Panská 7. ⓦ mucha.cz. Charge.

Alfons Mucha (1860–1939) made his name in turn-of-the-century Paris, where he shot to fame after designing Art Nouveau posters for the actress Sarah Bernhardt. "Le Style Mucha" became all the rage, but the artist himself came to despise this "commercial" period of his work, and, in 1910, Mucha moved back to his homeland and threw himself into the national cause, designing patriotic stamps, banknotes and posters for the new republic. The whole of Mucha's career is covered in the **permanent exhibition**, and an excellent video (in English) covers the decade of his life he devoted to the cycle of nationalist paintings known as the Slav Epic.

Museum of Communism (Muzeum komunismu)

MAP PAGE 82, POCKET MAP H12
V Celnice 4.
ⓦ muzeumkomunismu.cz. Charge.

Above a casino, on the first floor of the Savarin Palace, the **Museum of Communism** gives a brief rundown of twentieth-century Czech history, accompanied by a superb collection of Communist statues, film footage and propaganda posters. The politics are a bit simplistic – the popular postwar support for the party is underplayed – but it's worth tracking down for the memorabilia.

Powder Tower (Prašná brána)

MAP PAGE 82, POCKET MAP H12
Nám. Republiky 5. Charge.

Jindříšská věž

One of the eight medieval gate-towers that once guarded Staré Město, the **Powder Tower** was begun by King Vladislav Jagiello in 1475, shortly after he'd moved into the royal court, which was situated next door at the time. Work stopped when he retreated to the Hrad to avoid the wrath of his subjects; later on, it was used to store gunpowder – hence the name and the reason for the damage incurred in 1757, when it blew up. Most people, though, ignore the small historical exhibition inside, and climb straight up for the modest view from the top.

Obecní dům (Municipal House)

MAP PAGE 82, POCKET MAP H11–H12
Náměstí Republiky 5. Ⓦ obecnidum.cz.
Attached to the Powder Tower, and built on the ruins of the old royal court, the **Obecní dům** is by far the most exciting Art Nouveau building in Prague, one of the few places that still manages to conjure up the atmosphere of Prague's turn-of-the-twentieth-century café society. Conceived as a cultural centre for the Czech community, it's probably the finest architectural

achievement of the Czech national revival, extravagantly decorated inside and out by the leading Czech artists of the day. From the lifts to the cloakrooms, just about all the furnishings remain as they were when the building was completed in 1911.

The simplest way to soak up the interior – peppered with mosaics and pendulous brass chandeliers – is to have a coffee in the cavernous **café** (see page 87). For a more detailed inspection of the building's spectacular interior, you can sign up for one of the regular **guided tours** at the ground-floor information centre (charge).

Banka legií

MAP PAGE 82, POCKET MAP J11
Na poříčí 24.
The **Banka legií** (now a branch of the ČSOB) is one of Prague's most unusual pieces of corporate architecture. A Rondo-Cubist building from the early 1920s, it boasts a striking white marble frieze by Otto Gutfreund, depicting the epic march across Siberia undertaken by the Czechoslovak Legion and their embroilment in

Museum of Communism

Powder Tower and Municipal House on Republic Square

the Russian Revolution, set into the bold smoky-red moulding of the facade. You're free to wander into the main ground-floor banking hall, which retains its gently curved glass roof and distinctive red-and-white marble patterning.

Prague Museum

MAP PAGE 82, POCKET MAP K11/F5
Na poříčí 52. Ⓦ muzeumprahy.cz. Charge.
Nudging up to Prague's main coach station, a purpose-built neo-Renaissance mansion houses the excellent **Prague Museum**. Inside, there's an ad-hoc collection of the city's art, a smattering of antique bicycles, and usually an intriguing temporary exhibition on some aspect of the city.

The museum's prize possession, though, is Antonín Langweil's paper model of Prague which he completed in the 1830s. This is a fascinating insight into early nineteenth-century Prague – predominantly Baroque, with the cathedral incomplete and the Jewish quarter "unsanitized" – and, consequently, has served as one of the most useful records for the city's restorers. The most surprising thing, of course, is that so little has changed over the years.

Postal Museum (poštovní muzeum)

MAP PAGE 82, POCKET MAP J10
Nové mlýny 2.
Ⓦ postovnimuzeum.cz. Charge.
Housed in the **Vávrův dům**, an old mill near one of Prague's many water towers, the **Postal Museum** conceals a series of jolly nineteenth-century wall paintings of Romantic Austrian landscapes, and a collection of drawings on postman themes. The real philately is on the ground floor – a vast international collection of stamps arranged in vertical pull-out drawers. The Czechoslovak issues are historically and artistically interesting, as well as of appeal to collectors. Stamps became a useful tool in the propaganda wars of the last century; even such short-lived ventures as the Hungarian-backed Slovak Soviet Republic of 1918–19 and the Slovak National Uprising of autumn 1944 managed to print special issues. Under the First Republic, the country's leading artists, notably Alfons Mucha and Max Švabinský, were commissioned to design stamps, some of which are exceptionally beautiful.

Shops

Antikvariát dlážděná

MAP PAGE 82, POCKET MAP J12

Dlážděná 7. Ⓦ adplus.cz.

One of the city's longest-established and best secondhand bookstores, but it's the prints and original artwork that lure in shoppers.

Baťa

MAP PAGE 82, POCKET MAP H13

Václavské náměstí 6. Ⓦ bata.com.

Functionalist flagship store of Baťa shoe empire, with five floors of fancy footwear on Wenceslas Square.

Bontonland

MAP PAGE 82, POCKET MAP H13

Václavské náměstí 1.

In the *pasáž* on Wenceslas Square, Prague's biggest record store sells rock, folk, jazz and classical CDs, DVDs and video games.

Cellarius

MAP PAGE 82, POCKET MAP H13

Štěpánská 61. Ⓦ vinisto.cz.

Very well-stocked shop in the Lucerna *pasáž*, where you can taste and take away Czech wines.

Baťa's flagship store

Kotva

MAP PAGE 82, POCKET MAP H11

Náměstí Republiky 8. Ⓦ od-kotva.cz.

Prague's original 1970s department store has undergone a skin-deep makeover, taking the whole caboodle upmarket – and prices with it.

Moser

MAP PAGE 82, POCKET MAP H12

Na příkopě 12. Ⓦ moser.com.

A high-class emporium selling famous glass and crystal from West Bohemian spa town Karlovy Vary. Prices are high, but so is quality.

Palladium

MAP PAGE 82, POCKET MAP J11

Náměstí Republiky 1. Ⓦ palladiumpraha.cz.

The apotheosis of Czech consumerism, this is the country's largest shopping mall, occupying spruced-up former barracks opposite the *Obecní dům*.

Cafés

Dhaba Beas

MAP PAGE 82, POCKET MAP K11

Na poříčí 26. Ⓦ dhababeas.cz.

This Indian vegetarian self-service canteen is a very minimalist, 21st-century affair, set in a courtyard at the foot of an office block. The food – all pineapple fritters, chickpeas and basmati rice – is costed by weight, so the bill can add up faster than you think. Kč

Dobrá čajovna

MAP PAGE 82, POCKET MAP H13

Václavské náměstí 14.

Ⓦ dobracajovnapraha.cz.

Mellow yet rarefied teahouse, with an astonishing variety of teas (and a few Middle Eastern snacks) served by sandal-wearing waiters. Kč

Góvinda

MAP PAGE 82, POCKET MAP J10

Soukenická 27. Ⓦ govindarestaurace.cz.

Daytime Hare Krishna (Haré Kršna in Czech) restaurant with

The Art Nouveau interiors of *Imperial*

very basic decor, serving a menu of organic Indian veggie dishes. Kč

Imperial

MAP PAGE 82, POCKET MAP J11
Na poříčí 15. ⓦ **cafeimperial.cz.**
Built in 1914, and etched with incredible ceramic friezes on its walls, pillars and ceilings, the *Imperial* is a must for fans of outrageously sumptuous Art Nouveau decor. You can just come for a coffee, but it also serves breakfast, lunches and mains. KčKč

Lucerna

MAP PAGE 82, POCKET MAP H14
Vodičkova 36.
Wonderfully lugubrious fin-de-siècle café-bar on the first floor, en route to the cinema of the same name, with lots of faux marble and windows overlooking the Lucerna *pasáž*. Kč

Myšák

MAP PAGE 82, POCKET MAP H13
Vodičkova 31. ⓦ **mysak.ambi.cz.**
Stylish recreation of a famous and much-loved *cukrárna* that stood

on this spot in the interwar years. Expect a tantalizing selection of sweet treats like decadently high-stacked gateaux and the creamiest ice cream. Kč

Obecní dům

MAP PAGE 82, POCKET MAP H12
Náměstí Republiky 5.
The vast *kavárna*, with its iconic water fountain, is a glittering Art Nouveau period piece. The food is nice enough, but most folk come here to linger over a cup of coffee and a baked good from the tempting cake trolley. Kč

Pekářství moravec

MAP PAGE 82, POCKET MAP K10
Biskupský dvůr 1.
Rural Bohemia-style bakery, tucked away on a quiet square next to the relatively unvisited Church of sv Petra, selling a small selection of traditional cakes, freshly baked pastries, ice cream and excellent coffees. A great spot for an authentically early Czech breakfast. Kč

Restaurants

Hybernia

MAP PAGE 82, POCKET MAP J12
Hybernská 7. Ⓦ hybernia.cz.
Busy restaurant, with a nice outdoor terrace; specializes in *špízy* (needles), aka kebabs, but also serves good-value Czech food and pasta dishes. KčKč

Modrý zub (Blue Tooth)

MAP PAGE 82, POCKET MAP H13
Jindřišská 5. Ⓦ modryzub.com.
Good-value Thai rice and noodle dishes in a place that has a modern wine-bar feel to it – popular with Wenceslas Square shoppers. KčKč

Monarchie

MAP PAGE 82, POCKET MAP H14
Štěpánská 61. Ⓦ restaurace-monarchie.cz.
Imperial coats of arms line the walls at this interesting restaurant in the entrance to the Lucerna *pasáž*. The Austro–Bohemian menu includes Wiener schnitzel, suckling pig, and Pilsen goulash. KčKč

Pizza Nuova

MAP PAGE 82, POCKET MAP H11
Revoluční 1. Ⓦ pizzanuova.ambi.cz.
Big and stylish, this upstairs pizza and pasta place affords great views of the trams wending their way through Náměstí Republiky. KčKč

Plzeňská restaurace

MAP PAGE 82, POCKET MAP H11
Obecní dům, Náměstí Republiky 5.
ⓣ 222 002 780.
Located in the cellar of the Obecní dům, this is the country's most attractive Art Nouveau pub-restaurant, with exquisite tiling, wonderful stained glass and huge chandeliers. The menu celebrates the best of Czech meat dishes but is slightly overpriced, and portions are miserly. KčKčKč

TRITON

MAP PAGE 82, POCKET MAP H13
Václavské nám. 784/26.
Ⓦ prague-restaurant.eu.
Gourmet restaurant set in an unusual cave-like setting complete with stalactites. Go for the Czech Modern Art set menu and taste fine-dining twists on Czech classics (think truffle dumplings, slow-roasted veal, and a strudel quite unlike any you'll have ever seen before). KčKčKčKč

U sádlů

MAP PAGE 82, POCKET MAP H11
Klimentská 2. Ⓦ usadlu.cz.
Deliberately over-the-top themed medieval banqueting hall offering

Výtopna Railway Restaurant

a hearty Czech menu, with classics such as roast pork knuckle and goulash, helped down with lashings of frothing Budvar. KčKčKč

Výtopna Railway Restaurant

MAP PAGE 82, POCKET MAP J14
Václavské nám 802/56. Ⓦ vytopna.cz.
For something a bit different, why not have your meal delivered to your table by a small train? It might seem a bit gimmicky but it's a fun experience and the food is top notch (think hearty steaks, huge burgers and grilled meats). KčKčKč

Zvonice (Belltower)

MAP PAGE 82, POCKET MAP J12
Jindřišská. Ⓦ restaurantzvonice.cz.
Atmospheric but rather expensive restaurant crammed into the woodwork on the sixth and seventh floors of a medieval bell tower. Inventive mains include salmon roulade with ginger and lemongrass or grilled duck breast with a cherry and cardamom sauce. KčKčKčKč

Pub

Bredovský dvůr

MAP PAGE 82, POCKET MAP J13
Politických vězňů 12.
Ⓦ restauracebredovskydvur.cz.
Popular, brick-vaulted city pub, just off Wenceslas Square, serving standard pub food washed down with Pilsner Urquell or Velkopopovický Kozel.

Venues

Divadlo archa

MAP PAGE 82, POCKET MAP J11
Na poříčí 26. Ⓦ divadloarcha.cz.
The city's most innovative venue, with two versatile spaces, an art gallery and café. The programme of music, dance and theatre emphasizes new, experimental work, often with English subtitles or translation.

Kino Lucerna

Kino Lucerna

MAP PAGE 82, POCKET MAP H14
Vodičkova 36. Ⓦ kinolucerna.cz.
Grandiose 1909 cinema that eschews dubbed films and shows English-subtitled Czech films.

Lucerna Music Bar

MAP PAGE 82, POCKET MAP H14
Vodičkova 36. Ⓦ musicbar.cz.
Scruffy little basement bar that attracts some great musicians, local and touring, during the week, before descending into pop disco over the weekend.

Obecní dům – Smetanova síň

MAP PAGE 82, POCKET MAP H12
Náměstí Republiky 5. Ⓦ obecnidum.cz.
Fantastically ornate Art Nouveau concert hall which usually kicks off the Prague Spring International Music Festival and is home to the Prague Symphony Orchestra.

Prague State Opera (Státní opera Praha)

MAP PAGE 82, POCKET MAP J14
Wilsonova 4. Ⓦ narodni-divadlo.cz.
Sumptuous nineteenth-century opera house, originally built by the German-speaking community. It now hosts a programme of opera, ballet and drama performances.

Národní třída and southern Nové Město

Off the conventional tourist trail, and boasting only a few minor sights, the network of cobbled streets immediately to the south of Národní is nevertheless great to explore, as it harbours a whole range of interesting cafés, pubs, restaurants and shops. Southern Nové Město also boasts the city's finest stretch of waterfront, with a couple of leafy islands overlooked by magnificent nineteenth-century mansions that continue almost without interruption south to Vyšehrad.

Jungmannovo náměstí

MAP PAGE 91, POCKET MAP G13

Jungmannovo náměstí is named for **Josef Jungmann** (1772–1847), a prolific writer, translator and leading light of the Czech national revival, whose pensive, seated statue surveys the small, rather ill-proportioned square. The square itself boasts a couple of Czech architectural curiosities, starting with a unique **Cubist streetlamp** (and seat) from 1912, in the far eastern corner. The most imposing building is the chunky, vigorously sculptured **Palác Adria**, designed in Rondo-Cubist style in the early 1920s, with extra details added by Otto Gutfreund and a central *Seafaring* group by Jan Štursa. The building's *pasáž* (arcade) still retains its wonderful original portal featuring sculptures depicting the twelve signs of the zodiac. The theatre in the basement was the underground nerve centre of the 1989 Velvet Revolution, where the Civic Forum thrashed out tactics in the dressing rooms and gave daily press conferences in the auditorium against the stage set for Dürenmatt's *Minotaurus*.

Josef Jungmann statue on Jungmannovo náměstí

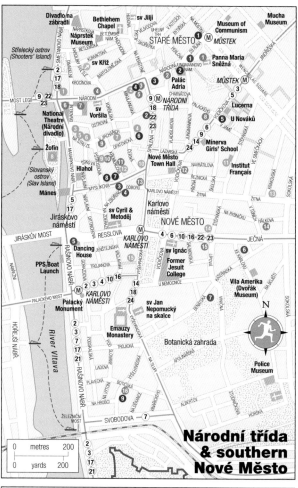

Národní třída & southern Nové Město

| 0 | metres | 200 |
| 0 | yards | 200 |

CAFÉS		PUBS & BARS		SHOPS	
Café 35 - Institut Français	11	Bar 23	9	Bazar	9
Café Louvre	2	Pivovarský dům	15	Čajový krámek	4
Café Slavia	1	U Fleků	10	Globe	8
Dante's Bistro	3	U havrana	14	Jan Pazdera	5
Marathon	10	U kruhu	8	Krakatit	2
My Raw	5	U pinkasů	1	MPM	7
Svatováclavská cukrárna	15	Vzorkovna Dog Bar	4	My národní	3
Velryba	4	Výloha Bar	16	Phono.cz	6
				Pylones	1

RESTAURANTS		CLUBS & VENUES		ACCOMMODATION	
Cicala	13	Divadlo Minor	12	Dancing House Hotel	5
Dynamo	6	Evald	2	Hotel 16	7
Pizzeria kmotra	7	Laterna magika	7	Hotel Jungmann	1
Střecha	12	MAT Studio	13	MadHouse	2
U Fleků	9	National Theatre	6	Mánes	3
U šumavy	14	Nebe	11	Miss Sophie's	6
Žofín Garden	8	Reduta	3	Mosaic House Design Hotel	4
		Rock Café	5		

Church of Panna Maria Sněžná

MAP PAGE 91, POCKET MAP H13
Jungmannovo náměstí 18.

Once one of the great landmarks of Wenceslas Square, **Panna Maria Sněžná** (St Mary-of-the-Snows) is now barely visible from the surrounding streets. To reach the church, go through the archway behind the statue of Jungmann, and across the courtyard beyond. Founded in the fourteenth century as a Carmelite monastery by Emperor Charles IV, who envisaged a vast coronation church larger than St Vitus Cathedral, only the chancel was built before the money ran out. The result is curious – a church which is short in length, but equal to the cathedral in height. The 33m-high, prettily painted vaulting is awesome, as is the gargantuan gold and black Baroque main altar which almost touches the ceiling.

Národní třída

MAP PAGE 91, POCKET MAP F14–G13

It was on this busy boulevard, lined with shops, galleries, banks and clubs, that the Velvet

View from Střelecký ostrov

Revolution began. On **November 17, 1989**, a 50,000-strong student demonstration worked its way from Vyšehrad to Národní třída, aiming to reach Wenceslas Square in what the authorities deemed an illegal march. Halfway down the street, their way was barred by the Communist riot police. The students sat down and refused to disperse, some of them handing out flowers. Suddenly, without any warning, the police attacked, and what became known as the *masakr* (massacre) began. In actual fact, no one was killed, though it wasn't for want of trying by the riot police. Beneath the arches of Národní 16, there's a small symbolic bronze relief of eight hands reaching out for help – candles are lit here every November 17, now a Czech national holiday.

Further down Národní, on the right-hand side, is an eye-catching duo of Art Nouveau buildings. The first, at no. 7, was built for the **Prague Savings Bank** (pojišťovna Praha), hence the beautiful mosaic lettering above the windows advertising *život* (life insurance) and *kapital* (loans), as well as help with your *důchod* (pension) and *věno* (dowry). Next door, the slightly more ostentatious **Topičův dům**, headquarters of the official state publishers, provides the perfect accompaniment, with an ornate wrought-iron and glass canopy.

Café Slavia

MAP PAGE 91, POCKET MAP F13
Smetanovo nábřeží 2.

The **Café Slavia** (see page 98), opposite the National Theatre at the end of Národní třída, has been a favourite haunt of the city's writers, dissidents, artists and actors since the 1920s when the Czech avant-garde movement, **Devětsil**, used to hold its meetings here, recorded for posterity by Nobel prize-winning poet Jaroslav Seifert. Under the Communists, dissident (and later president) Václav Havel and his pals

Velvet Revolution Memorial on Národní třída

used to hang out here under the watchful eye of state security agents. The ambience is not what it once was, and service can be quite gruff, but it still has a great riverside view and Viktor Oliva's classic *Absinthe Drinker* canvas on the wall.

Střelecký ostrov (Shooters' Island)

MAP PAGE 91, POCKET MAP E13–E14
Most Legií (Legion's Bridge).

The **Střelecký ostrov** is where the army held their shooting practice, on and off, from the fifteenth until the nineteenth century. Closer to the other bank, and accessible via **Most Legií** (Legion's Bridge), it became a popular spot for a Sunday promenade, and still hums with activity, especially in summer. The first Sokol gymnastics festival was held here in 1882, and the first May Day demonstrations took place on the island in 1890.

National Theatre (Národní divadlo)

MAP PAGE 91, POCKET MAP F14
Národní 2. Ⓦ narodni-divadlo.cz.

Overlooking the Vltava is the gold-crested **National Theatre**, one of the proudest symbols of the Czech national revival of the nineteenth century. Refused money from the Habsburg state coffers, Czechs of all classes dug deep into their pockets to raise the funds.

After thirteen years of construction, in June 1881, the theatre opened with a premiere of Smetana's *Libuše*. In August of the same year, fire ripped through the building, destroying everything except the outer walls. Within two years, the whole thing was rebuilt and even the emperor contributed this time. The grand portal on the north side of the theatre is embellished with suitably triumphant allegorical figures, and, inside, every square centimetre is taken up with paintings and sculptures by leading artists of the Czech national revival. The building has just undergone renovation to restore it to its former glory.

Standing behind the old National Theatre, and in dramatic contrast with it, is the theatre's unattractive extension, the opaque glass box of the **Nová scéna**, completed in 1983. It's one of those buildings most Praguers love to hate (they

National Theatre, a proud symbol of the Czech national revival

have an unrepeatable nickname for it), though compared to much of Prague's Communist-era architecture, it's not that bad.

Just for the record, the lump of molten rock in the courtyard is a symbolic evocation entitled *My Socialist Country*.

Vodičkova

MAP PAGE 91, POCKET MAP G14–H13

Vodičkova is probably the most impressive of the streets that head south from Wenceslas Square. Of the handful of buildings worth checking out along the way, the most remarkable of them all is **U Nováků** with its mosaic of bucolic frolicking and its delicate, ivy-like wrought ironwork – look out for the curious frog-prince holding up a windowsill. Further down the street stands the imposing neo-Renaissance **Minerva** girls' school, smothered in bright red sgraffito.

Founded in 1866, it was the first such institution in Prague, and notorious for the scandalous antics of its pupils, the "Minervans", who shocked bourgeois Czech society by experimenting with fashion, drugs and sexual freedom.

Karlovo náměstí

MAP PAGE 91, POCKET MAP G15

The impressive proportions of **Karlovo náměstí**, once Prague's biggest square, are no longer so easy to appreciate, obscured by trees and sliced in two by a busy thoroughfare. It was created by Emperor Charles IV as Nové Město's cattle market and used by him for the annual public display of his impressive (and grisly) collection of saintly relics. Now, it signals the southern limit of the city's main commercial district and the beginning of predominantly residential Nové Město.

Nové Město Town Hall (Novoměstská radnice)

MAP PAGE 91, POCKET MAP G14

Karlovo náměstí 23. Ⓦ nrpraha.cz. Charge.

Built in the fourteenth century, the **Nové Město Town Hall** is one of the finest Gothic buildings in the city, sporting three impressive triangular gables embellished with intricate blind tracery. It was here that Prague's **first defenestration** took place on July 30, 1419, when the radical Hussite preacher Jan Želivský and his penniless religious followers stormed the building, mobbed the councillors and burghers, and threw twelve or thirteen of them (including the mayor) out of the town hall windows onto the pikes of the Hussite mob below, who clubbed any survivors to death. Václav IV, on hearing the news, suffered a stroke and died just two weeks later. So began the long and bloody Hussite Wars.

After the amalgamation of Prague's separate towns in 1784, the building was used solely as a criminal court and prison. Nowadays, you can visit the site of the defenestration, and climb to the top of the tower for a view over central Prague. The town hall also puts on temporary art exhibitions.

Church of sv Ignác

MAP PAGE 91, POCKET MAP G15
Karlovo náměstí.

Begun in 1665, this former **Jesuit church** is quite remarkable inside, a pink and white confection, with lots of frothy stucco work and an exuberant pulpit dripping with gold drapery, cherubs and saints. The statue of St Ignatius (sv Ignác), which sits above the entrance surrounded by a sunburst, caused controversy at the time, as until then only the Holy Trinity had been depicted in such a way.

Cathedral of sv Cyril and Metoděj (Heydrich Martyrs' Memorial)

MAP PAGE 91, POCKET MAP F15
Corer of Resslova and Na Zderaze.

Amid all the traffic, it's extremely difficult to imagine the scene outside Prague's **Orthodox cathedral** on June 18, 1942, when seven Czechoslovak secret agents were besieged in the church by hundreds of SS troops. The agents had pulled off the dramatic assassination of Nazi leader **Reinhard Heydrich**, but had been betrayed by one of their own men. The Nazis surrounded the church just after 4am and fought a pitched battle for over six hours, trying explosives, flooding and any other method they could think of to drive the men out of their stronghold in the crypt. Eventually, all seven agents died by suicide rather than give themselves up.

There's a plaque at street level on the south wall to commemorate those who died, and an exhibition inside – you can also visit the crypt itself, which has been left pretty much as it was at the time.

Slovanský ostrov (Slav Island)

MAP PAGE 91, POCKET MAP E14–F15
Masarykovo nábřeží.

Slovanský ostrov is commonly known as **Žofín**, after the island's very yellow cultural centre, built in 1835 and named for Sophie, the mother of Emperor Franz-Josef I. By the late nineteenth century the island had become one of the city's foremost pleasure gardens. Even today, concerts, balls and other social gatherings take place here, and rowing boats can be rented in the summertime.

Tower of Nové Město Town Hall

Poised at the island's southern tip stands the onion-domed **Šítek water tower** and, spanning the narrow channel between the island and the riverside embankment, the **Mánes** art gallery, a striking, white functionalist box designed in 1930. At the northern end is a bronze statue of the best-known Czech female writer, Božena Němcová.

Dancing House (Tančící Dům)

MAP PAGE 91, POCKET MAP F15
Rašínovo nábřeží 80.

Designed by architect powerhouse duo Frank O. Gehry and Vlado Milunič, this striking building is known as the **Dancing House** (Tančící dům) or "Fred and Ginger building", after the sinuous shape of the building's two towers, which look vaguely like a couple engaged in ballroom dancing.

The apartment block next door was built at the start of the twentieth century by Václav Havel's grandfather, and was where, until the early 1990s, Havel and his first wife, Olga, lived in the top-floor flat.

Palacký Monument

MAP PAGE 91, POCKET MAP D7
Palackého náměstí.

The **Monument to František Palacký**, the nineteenth-century Czech historian, politician and nationalist, is an energetic and inspirational Art Nouveau sculpture from 1912. Ethereal bronze bodies, representing the world of the imagination, shoot out at all angles, contrasting sharply with the plain stone mass of the plinth, and below, the giant seated figure of Palacký, representing the real world.

Emauzy monastery

MAP PAGE 91, POCKET MAP D8
Vyšehradská 49. ⓦ emauzy.cz. Charge.

The intertwined concrete spires of the **Emauzy monastery** are an unusual modern addition to the Prague skyline. The monastery was one of the few important historical buildings to be damaged in World War II, in this case by a stray Anglo–American bomb (the pilot thought he was over Dresden). Founded by Emperor Charles IV, the cloisters contain some very valuable Gothic frescoes.

Dancing House, the brainchild of Frank O. Gehry and Vlado Milunič

Shops

Bazar

MAP PAGE 91, POCKET MAP D8
Vyšehradská 8.
This junk shop south of the city centre sells a huge range of odds and ends – everything from socialist-era pin badges to 1960s lightshades, and from 1980s Czechoslovak toy cars to German-built wardrobes.

Čajový krámek

MAP PAGE 91, POCKET MAP G13
Národní 20.
A colourful emporium stocking an amazing range of teas from all over the tea-growing and tea-drinking world, loose in big glass jars as well as bagged and boxed. Czechs don't tend to be big tea drinkers, but the fruit infusions here are very popular.

Globe

MAP PAGE 91, POCKET MAP F15
Pštrossova 6.
The expat bookshop par excellence – both a social centre (open until late) and a superbly well-stocked store with friendly staff.

Jan Pazdera

MAP PAGE 91, POCKET MAP H14
Vodičkova 28.
A spectacular edit of old and new cameras, microscopes, telescopes, opera glasses and binoculars.

Krakatit

MAP PAGE 91, POCKET MAP G13
Jungmannova 14.
This is big kids' nirvana – a little shop stuffed to the rafters with fantasy and military literature, plus a good range of science fiction and comics.

MPM

MAP PAGE 91, POCKET MAP F15
Myslíkova 19.
A whole range of kits for making model planes, tanks, trains, ships and cars, and toy soldiers.

Pylones

My Národní

MAP PAGE 91, POCKET MAP G13
Národní 26.
Once Prague's premier downtown department store, with the name a pun on its Communist predecessor (called *Máj*). It's actually owned by British supermarket behemoth Tesco, as the overspilling basement food hall attests.

Phono.cz

MAP PAGE 91, POCKET MAP G14
Patovická 24.
Miniscule vinyl shop, excellent for LPs from both western Europe and the former Czechoslovakia. Has a decent selection of the record players, too.

Pylones

MAP PAGE 91, POCKET MAP H13
28. října 11.
More like a museum of the weird and whimsical than a shop, filled to the rafters with colourful gadgets and gizmos for the office or home.

Cafés

Café 35 – Institut Français

MAP PAGE 91, POCKET MAP H14
Štěpánská 35.
Housed as it is in Prague's Institut Français, this is the spot for great coffee and fresh pastries – plus the chance to pose with a French newspaper. Kč

Café Louvre

MAP PAGE 91, POCKET MAP G13
Národní 22. ⓦ cafelouvre.cz.
Swish, turn-of-the-twentieth-century café with a long pedigree, still a popular stop for shoppers. There are high ceilings, inexpensive food and cakes, a billiard hall and window seats overlooking Národní. KčKč

Café Slavia

MAP PAGE 91, POCKET MAP F13
Smetanovo nábřeží 2. ⓦ cafeslavia.cz.
This famous 1920s riverside café pulls in a mixed crowd from shoppers and tourists to old-timers and the pre- and post-theatre mob.

Come here for a cup of coffee and the view, but not the food or the service. KčKč

Dantes Bistro

MAP PAGE 91, POCKET MAP F14
Masarykovo nábř. ⓦ food-prague.eu.
Casual spot near the river for well-priced healthy breakfasts and filling lunches. This is a good spot for veggie options too. Kč

Marathon

MAP PAGE 91, POCKET MAP G14
Černá 9.
Self-styled "library café" in the university's 1920s-style religion faculty, hidden in the backstreets, south of Národní třída. Kč

My Raw

MAP PAGE 91, POCKET MAP F14
Na Struze 5. ⓦ myraw.cz.
Raw vegan café with a surprising brunch menu (crêpes with chocolate cream and berries, "scrambled eggs" with raw bread, and açaí bowls) and an eclectic lunch offering (beetroot burgers, noodle dishes, rainbow salads). If

Café Louvre, a popular pit stop for shoppers

you're looking for a break from the hearty meat-forward cuisine found elsewhere in Prague, this is the best way to do it. KčKč

Svatováclavská cukrárna

MAP PAGE 91, POCKET MAP D7
Václavská pasáž, Karlovo náměstí 6.
☏ 224 916 774.

Join the local pensioner posse for cheap Turkish coffee and strudel at this busy *cukrárna* (café-bakery) within the glass-roofed Václavská pasáž, an interwar shopping arcade well off the tourist trail. Kč

Velryba (The Whale)

MAP PAGE 91, POCKET MAP G14
Opatovická 24. ⓦ kavarnavelryba.cz.

This funky pub-café has been serving up budget-friendly meals, beer, strong coffee and art exhibitions to a studenty crowd for over two and a half decades – and it's still going strong. Kč

Restaurants

Cicala

MAP PAGE 91, POCKET MAP H15
Žitná 43. ⓦ trattoria.cz.

Very good family-run Italian basement restaurant specializing (mid-week) in fresh seafood. There's also a wide range of pasta and an appetizing antipasto selection. KčKč

Dynamo

MAP PAGE 91, POCKET MAP F14
Pštrossova 29. ⓦ dynamorestaurace.cz.

Fashionable little spot with eye-catching retro-1960s designer decor. Serves tapas, pasta, steaks and Czech dishes. KčKč

Pizzeria kmotra (Godmother)

MAP PAGE 91, POCKET MAP F14
V jirchářích 12. ⓦ kmotra.cz.

This inexpensive, brick-vaulted basement pizza place is popular, and justifiably so – if possible, book a table in advance. KčKč

Café Slavia

Střecha

MAP PAGE 91, POCKET MAP F14
Křemencova 7. ⓦ restauracestrecha.cz.

Veganized Czech classics are the speciality here. The menu is packed with meat- and dairy-free versions of everything from ribs in plum sauce to fried cheese. The restaurant works with the local community to employ and train those that have experienced homelessness, and you can also buy an extra meal at the bar for someone in need. KčKč

U Fleků

MAP PAGE 91, POCKET MAP F14
Křemencova 11. ⓦ ufleku.cz.

Authentic beer hall dishing up Czech classics, such as goulash and smoked pork neck with dumplings, and plenty of beer. Also, a good spot for a casual evening drink to a soundtrack of live music (see page 100). KčKč

U šumavy

MAP PAGE 91, POCKET MAP H15
Štěpánská 3. ⓦ usumavy.cz.

Authentically Bohemian restaurant sporting stencilled walls, high ceilings and antique furniture. The menu is a meaty feast of *svíčková* (sirloin in cream sauce), venison, beef goulash and roast pork, all served with fluffy dumplings and tankards of countryside lager. KčKč

Žofín Garden

MAP PAGE 91, POCKET MAP E14
Slovanský ostrov 226. ⓦ zofinrestaurant.cz.
On the island nearest the National Theatre, this tranquil place plates up upmarket Czech food such as venison tartar, cod in a butter sauce and grilled lamb. KčKčKč

Pubs and bars

Bar 23

MAP PAGE 91, POCKET MAP F14
Křemencova 149. ⓦ bar23.cz.
Friendly bar where the bartenders can rustle up just about any cocktail you desire – at a very good price too.

Pivovarský dům

MAP PAGE 91, POCKET MAP H15
Corner of Lipová/Ječná.
ⓦ pivo-dum.cz/en/home.
Busy microbrewery dominated by big, shiny copper vats, with an excellent selection of gorgeous light, mixed and dark unfiltered beer (plus

The National Theatre

banana, coffee and wheat varieties), as well as Czech pub dishes.

U Fleků

MAP PAGE 91, POCKET MAP F14
Křemencova 11. ⓦ en.ufleku.cz.
Famous medieval brewery where the unique dark 13° beer, Flek, has been brewed since 1499. Seats over five hundred at a go, serves short measures (0.4l), charges extra for the music and still you might have to queue. Visit just to sample the beer, which you're best off doing during the day.

U havrana (The Crow)

MAP PAGE 91, POCKET MAP J15
Hálkova 6. ⓦ u-havrana.cz.
The chief virtue of this ordinary and surprisingly respectable Czech pub is that it serves food and Velkopopovický Kozel beer until the wee hours.

U kruhu (The Wheel)

MAP PAGE 91, POCKET MAP H14
Palackého 6. ⓦ prazdrojmenu.cz/u-kruhu.
Proper Czech pub, serving Plzeň beers and Velkopovický Kozel, with its own garden courtyard out front.

U pinkasů

MAP PAGE 91, POCKET MAP H13
Jungmannovo náměstí 16. ⓦ upinkasu.com.
Famous as the pub where Pilsner Urquell was first served in Prague, it still offers excellent unpasteurized beer and classic Czech pub food.

Výloha Bar

MAP PAGE 91, POCKET MAP D8
Vyšehradská 12. ⓦ vylohabar.cz.
At the southern end of the Nové Město, this neighbourhood drinking den is great for hanging with locals, playing darts and watching the Czechs win at ice hockey. Next door to Prague's Toilet Museum.

Vzorkovna Dog Bar

MAP PAGE 91, POCKET MAP F13
Národní 339/11. ⓦ vzorkovna.biz.
A cavernous bar with a string of themed rooms, football tables and

live music. You pay an entrance fee at the door and the money goes towards drinks and food. It can get crowded but it's a great spot for a fun night out.

Clubs and venues

Divadlo minor

MAP PAGE 91, POCKET MAP G14
Vodičkova 6. Ⓦ minor.cz.
The former state puppet theatre puts on children's shows most days, plus adult shows on occasional evenings, sometimes with English subtitles.

Evald

MAP PAGE 91, POCKET MAP G13
Národní 28. Ⓦ evald.cz.
Prague's most central arthouse cinema shows a discerning selection of new releases interspersed with plenty of classics.

Laterna magika (Magic Lantern)

MAP PAGE 91, POCKET MAP G13
Nová scéna, Národní 4.
Ⓦ narodni-divadlo.cz.
The National Theatre's Nová scéna, one of Prague's most modern and versatile stages, is the main base for Laterna magika, founders of multimedia and "black light" theatre in 1958. Its slick productions continue to effortlessly pull in crowds of curious tourists.

MAT Studio

MAP PAGE 91, POCKET MAP G15
Karlovo náměstí 19, entrance on Odborů.
Ⓦ mat.cz.
Tiny café and cinema popular with the film crowd, with an eclectic programme of shorts, documentaries and Czech films with English subtitles.

National Theatre (Národní divadlo)

MAP PAGE 91, POCKET MAP F14
Národní 2. Ⓦ narodni-divadlo.cz.
The living embodiment of the Czech national revival movement,

U Fleků has brewed beer since 1499

the National Theatre is worth visiting for the decor alone (see page 93). Czech plays are core to the repertoire, but there's also ballet and English-subtitled opera.

Nebe (Heaven)

MAP PAGE 91, POCKET MAP F14
Křemencova 10. Ⓦ nebepraha.cz.
A simple, well-proven formula: a snaking, brick-vaulted cocktail bar with a long cocktail menu and DJs that pump out dance music from the past four decades.

Reduta

MAP PAGE 91, POCKET MAP G13
Národní 20. Ⓦ redutajazzclub.cz.
Prague's best-known jazz club – Bill Clinton played his sax here in front of Havel – attracts a touristy crowd, but also some decent acts.

Rock Café

MAP PAGE 91, POCKET MAP G13
Národní 20. Ⓦ rockcafe.cz.
Not to be confused with the *Hard Rock Café*, this place is a stalwart of the live music scene; the basement stage showcases mostly new and emerging Czech bands.

Vyšehrad, Vinohrady and Žižkov

South of the city centre, the fortress of Vyšehrad makes for a perfect afternoon escape away from the human congestion of the Old and New towns: its illustrious cemetery shelters the remains of Bohemia's artistic elite; the ramparts afford superb views over the river; and beneath the fortress are several interesting examples of Czech Cubist architecture. The gentrified suburb of Vinohrady, to the east, is a late nineteenth-century residential neighbourhood, dominated by long streets of grandiose apartment blocks, with one or two specific sights to guide your wandering. By contrast, Žižkov, further north, is a grittier working-class district, whose shabby streets contain many pubs and clubs. The highlight here is the National Monument, a must for fans of Eastern European history.

Cubist villas

MAP PAGE 103, POCKET MAP D8

Even if you harbour only a passing interest in modern architecture, it's worth seeking out the cluster of **Cubist villas** beneath the fortress in Vyšehrad. The most impressive example is the apartment block at **Neklanova 30**, begun in 1913, which brilliantly exploits its angular location. Further along Neklanova, at no. 2, there's another Cubist facade, and around the corner is the most ambitious of the lot, the **Kovařovicova vila** (Libušina 49), which uses prism shapes and angular lines to produce the sharp geometric contrasts of light and dark shadows characteristic of Cubist painting.

The Cubist prisms of Kovařovicova vila

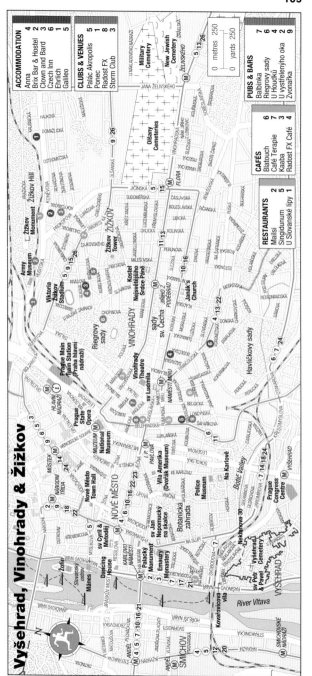

Vyšehrad, Vinohrady & Žižkov

Getting to Vyšehrad

To reach Vyšehrad, take tram #2, #3, #7, #14, #17, #18, #21 or #24 to Výtoň, and either wind your way up Vratislavova to the Cihelná brána or take the steep stairway from Rašínovo nábřeží that leads up through the trees. Alternatively, from Vyšehrad metro station, walk west past the ugly Prague Congress Centre, and enter via V pevnosti, where there's an information centre.

Vyšehrad

MAP PAGE 103, POCKET MAP D9
V pevnosti 5b. ⓦ praha-vysehrad.cz. Free.

The rocky red-brick fortress of **Vyšehrad** – literally "High Castle" – has more myths attached to it than any other place in Bohemia. According to Czech legend, this is the place where the Slavs first settled in Prague and where the chieftain Krok built a castle, whence his youngest daughter Libuše went on to found Praha itself. Alas, the archeological evidence doesn't really bear this claim out. What you see now are the remains of a fortified barracks built by the Habsburgs and then turned into a public park.

You can explore the fortress's northern entrance, or **Cihelná brána** (free), and the adjacent

Vyšehrad, or "High Castle"

dungeons, or **kasematy** (charge). After a short tour of a section of the underground passageways beneath the ramparts, you enter a vast storage hall, which conceals a smattering of the original statues from Charles Bridge, and, when the lights are switched off, reveals a camera obscura image of a tree.

Over in the southwestern corner of the fortress, in the **Gothic cellar** (charge); there's also a permanent exhibition on the history of Vyšehrad. The rock's big moment in Czech history was in the eleventh century when Přemysl Vratislav II – the first Bohemian ruler to bear the title "king" – built a royal palace here to get away from his younger brother who was lording it in the Hrad. Within half a century, the royals had moved back to Hradčany, into a new palace, and from then on Vyšehrad began to gradually lose its political significance.

Church of sv Petr and Pavel

MAP PAGE 103, POCKET MAP D9
K rotundě 10. Charge.

The twin openwork spires of this blackened sandstone church, rebuilt in the 1880s in neo-Gothic style on the site of an eleventh-century basilica, are now the fortress's most familiar landmark. Inside, you can admire the church's **Art Nouveau murals**.

Vyšehrad Cemetery (Vyšehradský hřbitov)

MAP PAGE 103, POCKET MAP D9
ⓦ slavin.cz.

Most Czechs come to Vyšehrad to pay a visit to the **cemetery**. It's

The Church of sv Petr and Pavel

a measure of the part that artists and intellectuals played in the foundation of the nation, and the regard in which they are still held, that the most prestigious graveyard in the city is given over to them: no soldiers, no politicians – not even the Communists managed to muscle their way in here (except on artistic merit). Sheltered from the wind by its high walls, lined on two sides by delicate arcades, it's a tiny cemetery filled with well-kept graves, many of them designed by the country's leading sculptors.

To the uninitiated, only a handful of figures are well known, but for the Czechs the place is alive with great names (there's a useful plan of the most notable graves at the entrance nearest the church). Ladislav Šaloun's grave for **Dvořák**, tucked beneath the arches, is one of the more showy ones, with a mosaic inscription, studded with gold stones, glistening behind wrought-iron railings.

Smetana, who died twenty years earlier, is buried in comparatively modest surroundings near the **Slavín monument**, the cemetery's focal point, which is the communal resting place of more than fifty Czech artists, including the painter Alfons Mucha and the opera singer Ema Destinová.

The grave of the Romantic poet Karel Hynek Mácha was the assembly point for the demonstration on November 17, 1989, which triggered the Velvet Revolution. This was organized to commemorate the fiftieth anniversary of the Nazi closure of Czech higher education institutions. A 50,000-strong crowd gathered here and attempted to march to Wenceslas Square, reaching as far as Národní before being beaten back (see page 92).

Police Museum

MAP PAGE 103, POCKET MAP E8
Ke Karlovu 1, Ⓜ Karlovo náměstí.
Ⓦ **muzeumpolicie.cz. Charge.**
The former Augustinian monastery of Karlov houses the **Police Museum**, which concentrates on road and traffic offences, and the force's latest challenges: forgery, drugs and murder. There's a whole section on the old Iron Curtain and espionage, but not a huge amount of information in English.

Dvořák Museum, dedicated to the iconic Czech composer

If you've got kids, however, they might enjoy driving round the mini-road layout on one of the museum trikes.

Na Karlově church

MAP PAGE 103, POCKET MAP E8
Ke Karlovu, Ⓜ Karlovo náměstí.
Founded by Emperor Charles IV and designed in imitation of Charlemagne's tomb in Aachen, this octagonal church is quite unlike any other in Prague. If it's open, you should take a look at the dark interior, which was remodelled in the sixteenth century by Bonifaz Wohlmut. The stellar vault has no central supporting pillars – a remarkable feat of engineering for its time, and one which gave rise to numerous legends about the architect being in league with the Devil.

Vila Amerika (Dvořák Museum)

MAP PAGE 103, POCKET MAP E7
Ke Karlovu 20, Ⓜ I. P. Pavlova. Charge.
The russet-coloured **Vila Amerika** was originally named after the local pub, but is now a museum devoted to **Antonín Dvořák** (1841–1904),

the most famous of all Czech composers, who lived for a time on nearby Zitná. Even if you've no interest in Dvořák, the villa itself is a delight, built as a Baroque summer house from around 1720. The tasteful period rooms, with the composer's music wafting in and out, and the tiny garden dotted with Baroque sculptures, together go a long way towards compensating for what the display cabinets may lack.

Náměstí Míru

MAP PAGE 103, POCKET MAP F7
If Vinohrady has a centre, it's the leafy square of **Náměstí Míru**, a good introduction to this neighbourhood. The most flamboyant building here is the **Vinohrady Theatre** (Divadlo na Vinohradech), built in 1907, with both Art Nouveau and neo-Baroque elements. Completely dominating the centre of the square is the brick basilica of **sv Ludmila**, designed in the late 1880s in a severe neo-Gothic style by the great neo-Gothicizer Josef Mocker, though the interior has the odd flourish of Art Nouveau.

In front a statue commemorates the **Čapek brothers**, writer Karel and painter Josef, local residents who together symbolized the golden era of the interwar republic. Karel died of pneumonia in 1938, while Josef perished in Belsen seven years later.

Kostel Nejsvětějšího Srdce Páně

MAP PAGE 103, POCKET MAP G7
Náměstí Jiřího z Poděbrad,
Ⓜ Jiřího z Poděbrad.

Prague's most-celebrated modern church, **Nejsvětějšího Srdce Páně** (Church of the Most Holy Heart of Our Lord) was built in 1928 by the Slovene architect **Josip Plečnik**. It's a marvellously eclectic work, employing a sophisticated potpourri of architectural styles: a Neoclassical pediment and a great slab of a clock tower with a giant transparent face in imitation of a Gothic rose window, as well as the bricks and mortar of contemporary constructivism.

Plečnik also had a sharp eye for detail – look out for the little gold crosses inset into the brickwork like stars, inside and out, and the celestial orbs of light suspended above the congregation.

Žižkov TV Tower (Televizní věž)

MAP PAGE 103, POCKET MAP G6
Mahlerovy sady 1, Ⓜ Jiřího z Poděbrad.
Ⓦ towerpark.cz. Charge.

At 216m in height, the **Žižkov TV Tower** is Prague's tallest building. Close up, it's an intimidating futuristic piece of architecture, made all the more disturbing by the giant babies crawling up the sides, courtesy of artist **David Černý**. Begun in the 1970s in a desperate bid to jam West German television transmissions, the tower became fully operational only in the 1990s. In the course of its construction, however, the Communists saw fit to demolish part of a nearby **Jewish cemetery** that had served the community between 1787 and 1891; a small section survives to the northwest of the tower. Following a major **reconstruction**, the tower now features a café, restaurant, bar, observatory and even a one-room hotel.

Olšany cemeteries (Olšanské hřbitovy)

MAP PAGE 103, POCKET MAP H6–J6
Vinohradská, Ⓜ Flora.

The vast **Olšany cemeteries** were originally created for the victims

The Police Museum focuses on the history of the force

of the 1680 plague epidemic. The perimeter walls are lined with glass cabinets, stacked like shoeboxes, containing funeral urns and mementoes, while the graves themselves are a mixed bag of artistic achievements, reflecting the funereal fashions of the day as much as the character of the deceased. The cemeteries are divided into districts and criss-crossed with cobbled streets; at each gate there's a map.

The cemeteries' two most famous incumbents are an ill-fitting couple: **Klement Gottwald**, the country's first Communist president, whose remains were removed from the mausoleum on Žižkov Hill after 1989 and reinterred here; and **Jan Palach**, the philosophy student who set light to himself in 1969 in protest at the Soviet occupation. Over 750,000 people attended Palach's funeral, and in an attempt to put a stop to the annual vigils at his graveside, the secret police removed his body and reburied him in his hometown outside Prague. In 1990, Palach's body was returned to Olšany; you'll find his grave just to the east of the main entrance.

New Jewish Cemetery (Nový židovský hřbitov)

MAP PAGE 103, POCKET MAP K6
Izraelská 1, Ⓜ Želivského. Charge.
Founded in the 1890s, the **New Jewish Cemetery** was designed to last for a century, with space for 100,000 graves. It's a truly melancholy spot, particularly in the east of the cemetery, where large empty allotments wait in vain to be filled by the generation that perished in the Holocaust.

Most people come here to visit **Franz Kafka's grave**, which is located around 400m east along the south wall and signposted from the entrance. He is buried, along with his mother and father (both of whom outlived him), beneath a plain headstone; the plaque below is dedicated to the memory of his three sisters, who died in the concentration camps.

Žižkov Hill

MAP PAGE 103, POCKET MAP G5–H5
U památníku, bus #133, #175 or #207 from Ⓜ Florenc.
Žižkov Hill is the thin green wedge of land that separates Žižkov from Karlín, the grid-plan

Kostel Nejsvětějšího Srdce Páně

Žižka monument on Žižkov Hill

industrial district to the north. From its westernmost point, which juts out almost to the edge of Nové Město, is the definitive panoramic view over the city centre.

It was here, on July 14, 1420, that the Hussites enjoyed their first and finest victory at the **Battle of Vítkov**, under the inspired leadership of the one-eyed general, Jan Žižka (hence the name given to the district). Outnumbered by ten to one, Žižka and his fanatical troops thoroughly trounced the Bohemian king (and the Holy Roman Emperor Sigismund) and his papal forces.

Despite its totalitarian aesthetics, the giant concrete **Žižkov monument**, which graces the crest of the hill, was actually built between the wars as a memorial to the Czechoslovak Legion who fought against the Habsburgs in World War I – the gargantuan statue of the mace-wielding Žižka, which fronts the monument, is reputedly the world's largest equestrian statue.

The building was later used by the Nazis as an arsenal, and eventually became a Communist mausoleum. In 1990, the Communists were cremated and quietly reinterred in Olšany. The monument now houses a fascinating **museum** (Ⓦnm.cz, charge) on the country's twentieth-century history; there's also a Communist monument to the fallen of World War II and a café on top, with great views over Prague's suburbs.

Army Museum (Armádní muzeum)

MAP PAGE 103, POCKET MAP G5
U památníku 2, bus #133, #175 or #207 from Ⓜ Florenc. Ⓦ vhu.cz.

Guarded by a handful of unmanned tanks, howitzers and armoured vehicles, the **Army Museum** has a fascinating permanent exhibition covering the country's storied military history from 1914 to 1945.

A fairly evenly balanced account of both world wars in the museum includes in-depth coverage of an array of controversial subjects such as the contentious exploits of the Czechoslovak Legion, the Heydrich assassination and the 1945 Prague Uprising.

Cafés

Blatouch

MAP PAGE 103, POCKET MAP F7
Americká 17. Ⓦ blatouch.cz.
Unpretentious café in the heart of Vinohrady that predates the flashier establishments all around. Salads, toasted sandwiches, pastas and tortillas, many of them vegetarian, make up the extensive menu and there's Ferdinand beer from Benešov. Kč

Café Terapie

MAP PAGE 103, POCKET MAP D8
Na hrobci 3. Ⓦ cafeterapie.cz.
Small, simply furnished café that serves up healthy Mediterranean-influenced salads, sandwiches, toasties and a few hot dishes. Kč

Kaaba

MAP PAGE 103, POCKET MAP K14
Mánesova 20. ☎ 222 254 021.
This stylish ice-cream parlour attracts a young, cool crowd with its mismatched retro decor and fun flavours. Serves breakfast, light meals and sundaes. Kč

Blatouch is a stalwart on the culinary scene

Radost FX Café

MAP PAGE 103, POCKET MAP J15
Bělehradská 120. Ⓦ radostfx.cz.
The veggie dishes at this expat favourite are filling, and there's a weekend brunch, decadent decor and a dance soundtrack with live DJs at the weekend. Kč

Restaurants

Mailsi

MAP PAGE 103, POCKET MAP G6
Lipanská 1. Ⓦ mailsi.cz.
Friendly Pakistani place in Žižkov that's great for a curry, as hot as you can handle. There's a rare subcontinental grocery shop next door. KčKčKč

Singidunum

MAP PAGE 103, POCKET MAP F7
Bělehradská 92. ☎ 222 544 113.
Singidunum is Latin for Belgrade, and it's the hot-tempered cuisine of the Balkans you'll find at this atmospheric place. There are *čevapčiči* (kebabs), Adriatic pastas, Croatian *pršut* (ham) plus Macedonian and Montenegrin wines. KčKčKč

U slovanské lípy

MAP PAGE 103, POCKET MAP H5
Tachovské náměstí 6. Ⓦ uslovanskelipy.cz.
Žižkov's oldest tavern rustles up solid, no-nonsense Prague and Bohemian dishes in a wood-panelled dining room. Interesting guest ales on tap. KčKč

Pubs and bars

Balbinka

MAP PAGE 103, POCKET MAP K15
Balbínova 6.
This small "poet's" pub is cherished by its regulars, and rightly so. With nightly live music ranging from rock to country or folk, part of the charm is never knowing what you might encounter on a night out.

Norwegian band Hurra Torpedo at the Palác Akropolis

Riegrovy sady

MAP PAGE 103, POCKET MAP G6
Riegrovy sady.
A real slice of local life, a
neighbourhood park café-pub
whose beer terrace is perennially
popular, especially for big TV
sports events.

U houdků

MAP PAGE 103, POCKET MAP G6
Bořivojova 110. ⓦ uhoudku.com.
Friendly local pub right in the
heart of Žižkov, with a beer garden,
Kozel on tap and cheap and
cheerful Czech food.

U vystřeleného oka (The Shot-Out Eye)

MAP PAGE 103, POCKET MAP G5
U božích bojovníků 3.
Big, loud, heavy-drinking watering
hole with good (sometimes live)
indie rock and lashings of Měšťan
beer, plus absinthe chasers.

Zvonařka (The Bell)

MAP PAGE 103, POCKET MAP F8
Šafaříkova 1.
Not only is this pub smart
and modern, but it also has an
appealing summer terrace with
great views over the Nuselské
schody and Botič valley.

Clubs and venues

Palác Akropolis

MAP PAGE 103, POCKET MAP G6
Kubelíkova 27. ⓦ palacakropolis.cz.
This old Art Deco theatre is Žižkov's
most popular club venue – it's also
a great place to just have a drink or
a bite to eat, as well as checking out
the DJ nights or the live gigs.

Ponec

MAP PAGE 103, POCKET MAP G5
Husitská 24a. ⓦ divadloponec.cz.
Former cinema, now an innovative
dance venue and centre for the
annual Tanec Praha Dance Festival
in June.

Radost FX

MAP PAGE 103, POCKET MAP J15
Bělehradská 120. ⓦ radostfx.cz.
This spacious club is Prague's
longest-running all-round dance
venue, with house and techno
keeping the expats happy.

Storm Club

MAP PAGE 103, POCKET MAP H5
Tachovské nám. ⓦ stormclub.cz.
Two stages and a chill-out zone
complete this edgy club skewed
toward electronic music fans.

Holešovice

Tucked into a U-bend in the River Vltava, the late nineteenth-century suburb of Holešovice boasts two huge splodges of green: Letná, overlooking the city centre, and, to the north, Stromovka, Prague's largest public park, bordering the Výstaviště funfair and trade fairgrounds. A stroll through the park brings you to the Baroque chateau of Troja and the leafy zoo. Two important cultural hubs are located in Holešovice – the city's main museum of modern art, Veletržní Palace, and the DOX Centre for Contemporary Art. Very few tourists make it out here, but it's well worth the effort, if only to remind yourself that Prague doesn't begin and end at Charles Bridge.

Letná

MAP PAGE 113, POCKET MAP D4

A high plateau hovering above the city, the flat green expanse of the **Letná** plain has long been the traditional assembly point for invading and besieging armies. Under the Communists, it was used primarily for the annual May Day parades, during which thousands trudged past the Sparta Prague stadium, where the Communist leaders would salute from their giant red podium. It once boasted the largest **Stalin monument** in the world: a 30m-high granite sculpture portraying a procession of Czechs and Russians being led to Communism by the Pied Piper

Views of the city from Letná

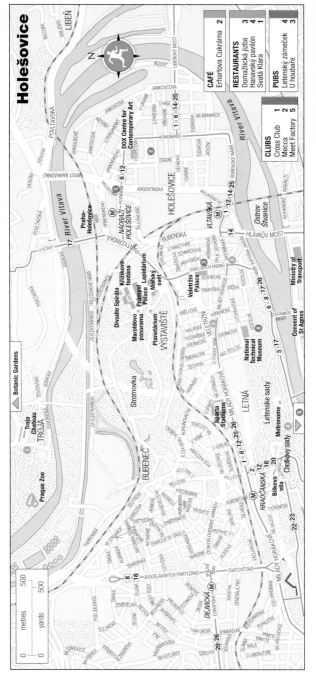

Holešovice

CAFÉ	
Erhartova Cukrárna	2

RESTAURANTS	
Domažlická jizba	3
Hanavský pavilon	4
Svatá Klara	1

PUBS	
Letenský zámeček	4
U houbaře	3

CLUBS	
Cross Club	1
Mecca	2
Meet Factory	5

National Technical Museum

figure of Stalin, but popularly
dubbed *tlačenice* (the crush)
because of its resemblance to a
Communist-era bread queue.
The monument was unveiled
on May 1, 1955, but within a
year Khrushchev had denounced
Stalin, and the monument was
blown up in 1962. On the site of
the Stalin statue, overlooking the
Vltava, stands a symbolic giant red
metronome (which is illuminated
at night).

Bílkova vila

MAP PAGE 113, POCKET MAP C4
Mieckiewiczova 1. Ⓦ ghmp.cz. Charge.
The **Bílkova vila**, an undervisited
branch of the Prague City Gallery,
honours one of the most original
of all Czech sculptors, **František
Bílek** (1872–1941). Built in
1911 to the artist's own design,
the house was intended as both a
"cathedral of art" and the family's
(rather lavish) home. The outside
is lined with columns reminiscent
of ancient Egypt; inside, Bílek's
extravagant religious sculptures
line the walls of his "workshop
and temple". In addition to his
sculptural and relief work in wood

and stone, often wildly expressive
and spiritually tortured, there are
also ceramics, graphics and a few
mementoes of Bílek's life. His living
quarters have also been restored
and have much of the original
wooden furniture, designed and
carved by Bílek himself, still in
place. Check out the dressing table
for his wife, shaped like some giant
church lectern, and the wardrobe
decorated with a border of hearts,
a penis, a nose, an ear and an eye
plus the sun, stars and moon.

Chotkovy sady

MAP PAGE 113, POCKET MAP C4
Prague's first public park, the
Chotkovy sady, was founded in
1833 by the ecologically minded
city governor, Count Chotek. The
atmosphere here is relaxed and you
can happily stretch out on the grass
and soak up the sun, or head for
the south wall, for an unrivalled
view of the bridges and islands of
the Vltava. At the centre of the
park there's a bizarre, melodramatic
grotto-like memorial to the
nineteenth-century Romantic
poet **Julius Zeyer**, an elaborate
monument from which life-sized

characters from Zeyer's works, carved in white marble, emerge from the blackened rocks.

National Technical Museum (Národní technické muzeum)

MAP PAGE 113, POCKET MAP E4
Kostelní 42. ⓦ ntm.cz. Charge.
Despite its dull name, the **National Technical Museum** is surprisingly interesting, with a showpiece hangar-like main hall containing an impressive gallery of Czech and foreign motorbikes, plus a wonderful collection of old planes, trains and automobiles from Czechoslovakia's industrial heyday between the wars – when the country's Škoda cars and Tatra soft-top stretch limos were really something to brag about. Other displays trace the development of early photography, while there's an excellent exhibit focusing on Czech architectural feats from the second half of the nineteenth century to the present, and a collection of some of Johannes Kepler and Tycho Brahe's astronomical instruments.

Veletržní palác (Trade Fair Palace)

MAP PAGE 113, POCKET MAP E3
Dukelských hrdinů 45.
ⓦ ngprague.cz. Charge.
The **Veletržní palác** gets nothing like the number of visitors it should. For not only does the building house Prague's best twentieth-century Czech and international art collection, it is also an architectural sight in itself. Built in 1928, the palace is Prague's ultimate functionalist masterpiece, particularly its vast white interior.

The gallery is bewilderingly big and virtually impossible to view in its entirety in a single visit. Temporary exhibitions are housed on the first and fifth floors, while the permanent collection occupies the other three. The popular **French art collection** includes works by Rodin, Renoir, Van Gogh, Matisse

and Picasso, while other notable **international** exhibits include cover Surrealist Miró, a couple of Henry Moore sculptures and a perforated Lucio Fontana canvas. There are also a few pieces by Klimt, Kokoschka, Schiele and Munch, whose influence on early twentieth-century Czech art was considerable.

The **Czech art** section starts with Impressionists Preisler and Slavíček, Cubists Čapek, Gutfreund, Filla and Kubišta, and a whole series of works by František Kupka, by far the most important Czech painter of the last century and (possibly) the first artist in the Western world to exhibit abstract paintings. **Socialist Realism** and **performance art** are not neglected either – plan on spending a full day here.

At the time of writing, the most talked-about exhibit was Mucha's Slav Epic (*Slovanská epopej*), a series of twenty oversized canvases painted between 1912 and 1928 following Alfons Mucha's return to his homeland from Paris. Having spent the Communist period in a disued chateau in Moravia, in the early 2000s the city of Prague decided the Slav Epic belonged

Gallery at the Veletržní palác

in the capital and the cycle now hangs in the Veletržní palác as a "temporary exhibition". Where it will go from here, if it ever does, no one knows.

DOX Centre for Contemporary Art

MAP PAGE 113, POCKET MAP G2
Poupětova 1. ⓦ dox.cz. Charge.

Founded by a private initiative with the goal of making Prague a major European centre for contemporary art, the **DOX Centre** presents mostly group exhibitions that aim to push boundaries and introduce new dialogues. Both Czech and international artists are represented, while the organization's educational programmes, debates and talks make it a pivotal part of the local arts scene. The sprawling building is stunning, too, and features a lovely café and good design shop.

Výstaviště (Exhibition Grounds)

MAP PAGE 113, POCKET MAP E2
Dukelských hrdinů.
ⓦ vystavistepraha.eu. Charge.

Since the 1891 Prague Exhibition, **Výstaviště** has served as the city's main trade fair arena and funfair. At the centre of the complex is the flamboyant stained-glass and wrought-iron **Průmysl Palace**, scene of Communist Party rubber-stamp congresses. Several modern structures were built for the 1991 Prague Exhibition, including a circular theatre, **Divadlo Spirála**.

The grounds are busiest at the weekend, particularly in summer, when hordes of Prague families descend to munch hot dogs and drink beer. Apart from the annual trade fairs and special exhibitions, there are a few permanent attractions: the city's **Planetárium** (ⓦplanetarium.cz; charge), which has static displays and shows films; the **Maroldovo panorama** (charge), a giant diorama of the 1434 Battle of Lipany; and **Mořský svět** (ⓦmorsky-svet. cz; charge), an aquarium full of colourful tropical fish, a few rays and some sea turtles.

In the long summer evenings, the *Pražon* restaurant shows outdoor films and hosts concerts, and there are hourly evening performances (charge) by the dancing **Křižík Fountain**, devised for the 1891

The Baroque Troja chateau was designed by Jean-Baptiste Mathey

Getting to Troja and the zoo

To reach Troja and the zoo, you can either **walk** from Výstaviště, catch **bus** #112, which runs frequently from metro Nádraží Holešovice, or take a **boat** (ⓦparoplavba.cz; charge) from the PPS landing place on Rašínovo nábřeží, metro Karlovo náměstí.

Exhibition by the Czech inventor František Křižík. Call ☎220 103 224 for details.

Lapidárium

MAP PAGE 113, POCKET MAP E2
U Výstaviště. ⓦnm.cz. Charge.
Official depository for the city's sculptures which are under threat either from demolition or from the weather, the **Lapidárium** houses a much-overlooked collection, ranging from the eleventh to the nineteenth century. Some of the statues saved from the perils of Prague's polluted atmosphere, such as the bronze equestrian statue of St George, will be familiar if you've visited Prague Castle before; others, such as the figures from the towers of Charles Bridge, were more difficult to inspect closely in their original sites. Many of the original statues from the bridge can be seen here, including the ones that were fished out of the Vltava after the flood of 1890.

One outstanding sight is what remains of the **Krocín fountain**, a highly ornate Renaissance work in red marble, which used to grace Staroměstské náměstí (see page 60). Several pompous imperial monuments that were bundled into storage after the demise of the Habsburgs in 1918 round off the museum's collection. By far the most impressive is the bronze statue of Marshal Radecký, scourge of the 1848 revolution, carried aloft on a shield by eight Habsburg soldiers.

Stromovka

MAP PAGE 113, POCKET MAP D2
Originally laid out as hunting grounds for the noble occupants of the castle, **Stromovka** is now

Prague's largest and leafiest public park. If you're heading north for Troja and the city zoo, a stroll through the park is by far the most pleasant approach. If you want to explore a little more of it, head west, sticking to the park's southern border, and you'll eventually reach a neo-Gothic former royal hunting chateau, which served as the seat of the Governor of Bohemia until 1918.

Troja chateau (Trojský zámek)

MAP PAGE 113, POCKET MAP C1
U trojského zámku 1. ⓦghmp.cz. Charge.
The **Troja chateau** was designed by Jean-Baptiste Mathey for the powerful Šternberg family towards the end of the seventeenth century. The best features of the rust-coloured Baroque facade are the monumental balustrades, where

Julius Zeyer memorial in Chotkovy sady

blackened figures of giants and titans battle it out. The star exhibits are the gushing frescoes depicting the victories of the Habsburg Emperor Leopold I (who reigned from 1657 to 1705) over the Turks, which cover every inch of the walls and ceilings of the grand hall. You also get to wander through the chateau's pristine, trendsetting, French-style formal gardens, the first of their kind in Bohemia.

Prague Zoo (Zoologická zahrada)

MAP PAGE 113, POCKET MAP C1
U trojského zámku 3.
Ⓦ zoopraha.cz. Charge.

Founded in 1931 on the site of one of Troja's numerous hillside vineyards, Prague's **zoo** has had a lot of money poured into it and now has some very imaginative enclosures. All the usual animals are on show here – including elephants, hippos, giraffes, zebras, big cats and bears – and kids, at least, will enjoy themselves. A bonus in the summer is the **chairlift** (*lanová dráha*) from the duck pond over the enclosures to the top of the hill, where the prize exhibits – a rare breed of miniature horse known as Przewalski – hang out. Other highlights include the red pandas, giant tortoises, Komodo dragons, and the bats that fly past your face in the Twilight Zone.

Botanic Gardens (Botanická zahrada)

MAP PAGE 113, POCKET MAP D1
Nádvorní 134. Ⓦ botanicka.cz. Charge.

Hidden in the woods to the north of the chateau, the city's **Botanic Gardens** feature a vineyard, a Japanese garden, several glasshouses and great views over Prague. Cradled among the trees a little higher up the hill, there's also a spectacular, curvaceous greenhouse, **Fata Morgana**, with butterflies flitting about amid the desert and tropical plants.

Airship Gulliver atop the DOX Centre for Contemporary Art

Café

Erhartova cukrárna

MAP PAGE 113, POCKET MAP E3
Milady Horákové 56.
Ⓦ erhartovacukrarna.cz.
First Republic sweet shop with
delectable cakes and a long queue.
The café's functionalist architecture
is a treat for the eyes as well. Kč

Restaurants

Domažlická jizba

MAP PAGE 113, POCKET MAP E3
Strossmayerovo náměstí 2.
Ⓦ domazlicka-jizba.cz.
Join locals at this wood-panelled,
traditional dining room; it's been
banging down plates of goulash and
chicken schnitzel since 1906. KčKč

Hanavský pavilón

MAP PAGE 113, POCKET MAP E10
Letenské sady 173. Ⓦ hanavsky-pavilon.cz.
Highly ornate wrought-iron Art
Nouveau pleasure pavilion high
above the Vltava, with stunning
views from the terrace. KčKčKč

Svatá Klara (Saint Clare)

MAP PAGE 113, POCKET MAP C1
U trojského zámku 35. ☎ 233 540 173.
Formal restaurant, dating to 1679,
in a romantic wine cave. Excels in
fondues and game dishes. KčKčKč

Pubs and bars

Fraktal

MAP PAGE 113, POCKET MAP D3
Šmeralova 1. Ⓦ fraktal.cz.
Very popular cellar bar with ad-hoc
funky furnishings, exhibitions and
occasional live music, plus a beer
garden and kids' play area outside.

Letenský zámeček

MAP PAGE 113, POCKET MAP E4
Letenské sady. Ⓦ letenskyzamecek.cz.
The beer garden, with its great
views down the Vltava, is cheap and

Hanavský pavilón

popular with locals. The restaurant is
rather upmarket and less special.

U houbaře
(The Mushroom Picker)

MAP PAGE 113, POCKET MAP E3
Dukelských hrdinů 30. Ⓦ u-houbare.cz.
Comfortable local pub, directly
opposite the Veletržní palác, serving
Pilsner Urquell and inexpensive
Czech pub food.

Clubs and venues

Cross Club

MAP PAGE 113, POCKET MAP F2
Plynární 23. Ⓦ crossclub.cz.
Labyrinthine, multi-floor club
decked out in arty industrial decor,
located near Nádraží Holešovice. The
DJs on each floor range from techno
to ambient.

Mecca

MAP PAGE 113, POCKET MAP G2
U Průhonu 3. Ⓦ mecca.cz.
Despite being located out of
the way in Prague 7, this coolly
converted factory is one of the
most impressive and popular clubs
in the city.

Meet Factory

MAP PAGE 113, POCKET MAP C9
Ke Sklárně 15, Smíchov. Ⓦ meetfactory.cz.
Multipurpose cultural venue co-
founded by artist David Černý,
with regular concerts featuring
obscure overseas and Czech acts.
It's a way south of Holešovice, but
easy to reach on tram #12/20 from
Chotkovy sady.

ACCOMMODATION

The landmark facade of *Grand Hotel Bohemia*

Accommodation

Compared to the price of beer, accommodation in Prague is very expensive. If you're looking for a double and can pay around 3500Kč (€150) a night, then you'll find plenty of choice. At the other end of the scale, there are numerous hostels charging around 350Kč (€15) for a bed. However, there's a shortage of anything in between: you'll be hard-pressed to find decent, inexpensive to middle-range places. You can, however, get some very good deals – and undercut the often-exorbitant rack rates – by booking online well in advance. Given that Prague can be busy all year round, it's not a bad idea to book ahead in any case. All accommodation prices in this chapter are for the cheapest double room in high season; breakfast is usually included in the price, unless otherwise stated.

Hradčany

HOTEL LORETA MAP PAGE 34, POCKET MAP B11. **Loretánské náměstí 8, tram #22 to Pohořelec** Ⓦ **hotelloreta.cz.** This peaceful hotel, housed in a former riding school, features comfortable rooms with ornate furniture and painted ceilings. Great location for visiting the castle and the baroque Loreta monastery next door. KčKč

QUESTENBERK MAP PAGE 34, POCKET MAP A12. **Úvoz 15, tram #22 from** Ⓜ **Malostranská to Pohořelec** Ⓦ **questenberkhotel-prague.com.** From the outside, this hotel looks like a Baroque chapel, but inside it's been totally modernized. Rooms are smart but plain, though some take in superb views. Kč

SAVOY PRAGUE MAP PAGE 34, POCKET MAP A5. **Keplerova 6, tram #22 from** Ⓜ **Malostranská to Pohořelec** Ⓦ **savoyprague.cz.** Dated, charming luxury hotel on Hradčany's western edge, still sporting its original Art Nouveau facade. Popular for its marble bathrooms and free minibar, there's also a lovely lounge area. Breakfast extra. KčKčKč

U KRÁLE KARLA (KING CHARLES) MAP PAGE 34, POCKET MAP B11. **Úvoz 4, tram #22 to Pohořelec** Ⓦ **axxoshotels.com/the-king-charles.** Possibly the most tastefully exquisite of all the small luxury hotels in the castle district, adorned with beautiful antique furnishings and stained-glass windows. Situated at the top of Nerudova,

Accommodation price codes

All the accommodation detailed in this Guide has been graded according to the four price categories listed below. These represent how much you can expect to pay in each establishment for the least expensive double or twin room with breakfast in high season.

Kč	Kč1190–2860 (€50–120)
KčKč	Kč2880–3570 (€121–150)
KčKčKč	Kč3590–4760 (€151–200)
KčKčKčKč	Kč4780 (€201+)

it's a steep calf-busting walk from the nearest tram stop, however. KčKč

U RAKA (THE CRAYFISH) MAP PAGE 34, POCKET MAP A10. Černínská 10, tram #22 from Ⓜ Malostranská to Brusnice Ⓦ hoteluraka.cz. The perfect hideaway, six double rooms in a little half-timbered, eighteenth-century cottage in Nový Svět. No children under 12 or dogs, and advance reservation a must. KčKčKč

Malá Strana

ALCHYMIST GRAND HOTEL MAP PAGE 42, POCKET MAP C12. Tržiště 19, tram #12, #20 or #22 to Malostranské náměstí Ⓦ alchymisthotel.com. Total decadent luxury abounds in this sixteenth-century palace, which has been tastefully converted into a secluded spa hotel, complete with Indonesian massages and an indoor swimming pool. KčKčKčKč

ARIA MAP PAGE 42, POCKET MAP C12. Tržiště 9, tram #12, #20 or #22 to Malostranské náměstí Ⓦ ariahotel.net. A popular hotel with a clutch of musically themed rooms and a special music library. Guests can enjoy the stunning roof terrace and private access to one of Prague Castle's gardens. KčKčKčKč

DIENTZENHOFER MAP PAGE 42, POCKET MAP D12. Nosticova 2, tram #12, #20 or #22 to Hellichova Ⓦ dientzenhofer. cz. Birthplace of the eponymous architect Kilian Ignác Dientzenhofer and a very popular and unpretentious pension, as it's one of the few reasonably priced places (anywhere in Prague) to have wheelchair access and specially adapted rooms. Kč

DŮM U VELKÉ BOTY (THE BIG SHOE) MAP PAGE 42, POCKET MAP B12. Vlašská 30, tram #12, #20 or #22 to Malostranské náměstí Ⓦ dumuvelkeboty.cz. The sheer discreteness of this pension, in a lovely old building in the quiet backstreets, is one of its main draws. It's truly a home away from home, run by a very friendly couple, who speak good English. There is a series of cosy guest rooms, complete with genuine antiques and sumptuous fabrics; some are en suite. Breakfast is included. Kč

OREA PLACE CHARLES BRIDGE APARTHOTEL PRAGUE MAP PAGE 42, POCKET MAP D12. Míšenská 12, tram #12, #20 or #22 to Malostranské náměstí Ⓦ lokal-inn-prague.hotel-dir.com. Top-drawer boutique hotel (previously Lokal Inn) where the original features of the Baroque building have been preserved to provide a backdrop for the interesting design features. There is also a superb contemporary restaurant downstairs. KčKč

NERUDA MAP PAGE 42, POCKET MAP B11. Nerudova 44, tram #12, #20 or #22 to Malostranské náměstí Ⓦ designhotelneruda.com. This stylish hotel is a fair walk up Nerudova, but it has a funky, glass-roofed foyer, uses lots of cool natural stone, and boasts smart, minimalist modern decor in the rooms. KčKč

POD VĚŽÍ MAP PAGE 42, POCKET MAP D12. Mostecká 2, tram #12, #20 or #22 to Malostranské náměstí Ⓦ podvezi.com. One of Prague's best small hotels, a few steps from Charles Bridge, with understated but luxurious rooms. Restaurant on the premises (see page 52). KčKčKčKč

SAX MAP PAGE 42, POCKET MAP C12. Janský vršek 3, tram #12, #20 or #22 to Malostranské náměstí Ⓦ hotelsax. cz. Perfectly located in the backstreets off Nerudova, this hotel has gone for a remarkably convincing groovy retro 1960s look, but it's also a very well-run, well-equipped place with a DVD library. Kč

U PÁVA (THE PEACOCK) MAP PAGE 42, POCKET MAP E11. U lužického semináře 32 Malostranská Ⓦ hotel-upava.cz. Hidden away in the quiet backstreets, U Páva boasts some impressively over-the-top Baroque fittings – real and repro. Some rooms have views over to the castle, and service is good. KčKčKč

U ZLATÉ STUDNĚ (THE GOLDEN WELL) MAP PAGE 42, POCKET MAP D11. U zlaté studně 4, tram #12, #20 or #22 to Malostranské náměstí Ⓦ goldenwell.cz. A special location: tucked into the terraces below Prague Castle, next to the terraced gardens, with incredible views across the rooftops. Many of the rooms feature original ceilings, and there's a good restaurant with a wonderful summer terrace. KčKčKčKč

U ZLATÝCH NŮŽEK (THE GOLDEN SCISSORS) MAP PAGE 42, POCKET MAP E12. **Na Kampě 6, tram #12, #20 or #22 to Malostranské náměstí** Ⓦ uzlatychnuzek.cz. Ten rooms with parquet flooring, the odd beam and simple modern furnishings. On Kampa island, close to Charles Bridge. KčKč

Staré Město

ČERNÝ SLON (BLACK ELEPHANT) MAP PAGE 56, POCKET MAP G11. **Týnská 1** Ⓜ **Náměstí Republiky** Ⓦ hotelcernyslon.cz. Another ancient building tucked away off Old Town Square by the north portal of the Týn church, now tastefully converted into a very comfortable small hotel. KčKč

CLOISTER INN MAP PAGE 56, POCKET MAP F13. **Konviktská 14** Ⓜ **Národní třída** Ⓦ cloisterinnprague.com. Pleasant, well-equipped hotel in a former nunnery down one of the backstreets; the rooms are simply furnished with modern fittings, and the location is good. Kč

THE DOMINICAN MAP PAGE 56, POCKET MAP G12. **Jilská 235/7** Ⓜ **Národní** Ⓦ třídaaxxoshotels.com/the-dominican. Well-decorated rooms complete with comfy beds and en suites. Breakfast is excellent, and the chef is always happy to accommodate. KčKč

GRAND HOTEL BOHEMIA MAP PAGE 56, POCKET MAP H12. **Kralodvorská 4** Ⓜ **Náměstí Republiky** Ⓦ grandhotelbohemia.cz. Probably the most elegant luxury hotel in the Old Town, just behind the Obecní dům, with some very tasty Art Nouveau decor and all the amenities you'd expect from an Austrian outfit. KčKčKčKč

GRAND HOTEL PRAHA MAP PAGE 56, POCKET MAP G12. **Staroměstské náměstí 22** Ⓜ **Můstek** Ⓦ grandhotelpraha.cz. If you want a guest room overlooking the astronomical clock on Old Town Square, then book in here, well in advance. There are beautiful antique furnishings, big

oak ceilings, but only a very few rooms, including a single room and an attic suite sleeping up to four guests. KčKčKčKč

HAŠTAL MAP PAGE 56, POCKET MAP H11. **Haštalská 16** Ⓜ **Náměstí Republiky** Ⓦ hotelhastalprague.com. Opposite the sv Haštala church on peaceful Haštalské náměstí, this established hotel offers good value for money. Guest rooms sport dark-wood furniture and Prague-themed artwork, and the restaurant is an authentic piece of Art Nouveau. KčKčKč

HOTEL CLEMENTIN OLD TOWN MAP PAGE 56, POCKET MAP F12. **Seminářská 4.** Ⓜ **Staroměstská** Ⓦ clementin.cz. A great option smack bang in the centre of everything, with comfortable guest rooms and very helpful staff. KčKč

HOTEL U ČERVENÉ ŽIDLE MAP PAGE 56, POCKET MAP F12. **Liliová 4, tram #17 or #18 to Karlovy lázně** Ⓦ redchairhotel.com. Unassuming hotel on a pretty Old Town lane, offering thirteen rooms with green-stained timber furniture and high ceilings. There's a car park in the courtyard for anyone brave enough to drive into the Old Town's maze of streets. KčKčKčKč

JOSEF MAP PAGE 56, POCKET MAP H11. **Rybná 20** Ⓜ **Náměstí Republiky** Ⓦ hoteljosef.com. Prague's top design hotel exudes hipster professionalism; the lobby is a symphony in off-white efficiency and the rooms continue the crisply maintained minimalist theme with limestone showers and sharply pressed linens. KčKčKč

LIPPERT HOTEL MAP PAGE 56, POCKET MAP G12. **Mikulášská 2** Ⓜ **Staroměstská** Ⓦ lipperthotel.cz. So central it's ridiculous, yet with friendly and helpful staff. Guest rooms are well appointed, with hand-painted ceilings; some offer incredible views onto Old Town Square. For a good night's sleep, ask for one of the quieter pads at the back. KčKč

RESIDENCE ŘETĚZOVÁ MAP PAGE 56, POCKET MAP F12. **Řetězová 9** Ⓜ **Staroměstská** Ⓦ hotel-residence-retezova.pragueshotel.net/cs. Attractive apartments of all sizes, with kitchenettes, wooden or stone floors, Gothic vaulting or authentic wooden beams, and repro furnishings throughout. Kč

THE MOZART PRAGUE MAP PAGE 56, POCKET MAP F12. Karoliny Světlé 20 Ⓜ Národní třída Ⓦ themozart.com. Former Baroque palace turned luxury hotel in the heart of the Old Town, with charming and efficient staff; rooms and suites are decked out in an aesthetic blend of antique and repro furniture. KčKčKčKč

TÝN MAP PAGE 56, POCKET MAP H11. Týnská 19 Ⓜ Náměstí Republiky Ⓦ hostelpraguetyn.com. Prague's most central hostel is a funky but pretty basic affair, located in a quiet little courtyard within easy staggering distance of the Old Town Square. KčKč

U MEDVÍDKŮ (THE LITTLE BEARS) MAP PAGE 56, POCKET MAP G13. Na Perštýně 7 Ⓜ Národní třída Ⓦ umedvidku.cz. The rooms above this famous Prague pub are plainly furnished, quiet considering the locale, and therefore something of an Old Town bargain; booking ahead essential. Kč

UNITAS MAP PAGE 56, POCKET MAP F13. Bartolomějská 9 Ⓜ Národní třída Ⓦ unitas. cz. Occupying a former Franciscan convent, the *Unitas* offers simple and spacious double and twin rooms – though they are slightly overpriced. KčKčKčKč

U TŘÍ BUBNŮ (THE THREE DRUMS) MAP PAGE 56, POCKET MAP G12. U radnice 8–10 Ⓜ Staroměstská Ⓦ utribubnu.cz. Small hotel just off Old Town Square with five tastefully furnished rooms, either with original fifteenth-century wooden ceilings or lots of exposed beams. No lift but plenty of stairs. Kč

VENTANA MAP PAGE 56, POCKET MAP G12. Celetná 7 Ⓜ Náměstí Republiky Ⓦ ventana-hotel.net. Guests who stay at this super-central luxury boutique hotel rave about the spacious rooms, excellent breakfast and impeccably regimented staff. Add to this Prague's most stylish lobby, gleaming marble-and-tile bathrooms and a full library illuminated by crystal chandeliers, and the *Ventana* shapes up

as one of Prague's finest places to unpack your suitcase. KčKčKčKč

Wenceslas Square and northern Nové Město

ALCRON MAP PAGE 82, POCKET MAP H14. Štěpánská 40 Ⓜ Můstek or Muzeum Ⓦ radissonblu.com/en/hotel-prague. Giant 1930s luxury hotel, situated just off Wenceslas Square, superbly restored to its former Art Deco glory by the Radisson chain. Double rooms here are without doubt the most luxurious and tasteful you'll find in Nové Město. KčKčKčKč

BOHO PRAGUE MAP PAGE 82, POCKET MAP J12. Senovážná 4 Ⓜ Hlavní nádraží Ⓦ hotelbohoprague.com. Go boho in Bohemia at one of Prague's most stylish hotels, where guest rooms sport shades of grey you never knew existed. There's an in-house restaurant, plus a smattering of leisure facilities. KčKčKčKč

BOSCOLO PRAGUE MAP PAGE 82, POCKET MAP K12. Senovážné náměstí 13 Ⓜ Hlavní nádraží Ⓦ prague.boscolohotels.com. Occupying one of Prague's grandest city-centre palaces, this five-star abode has some incomparably swish public areas, a remarkable spa, rooms done out with Italian flair, and lots of facilities such as a fitness centre and a pool. KčKčKčKč

HARMONY MAP PAGE 82, POCKET MAP K11. Na Poříčí 31 Ⓜ Florenc Ⓦ hotelharmony.cz. For those on a budget, this is a very sound low-cost option. As an added advantage, it's only a dumpling's throw from the main sights. Good for those who want to sleep, shower and breakfast – for medieval grandeur, go elsewhere. Kč

HOSTEL ROSEMARY MAP PAGE 82, POCKET MAP J13. Růžová 5 Ⓜ Můstek or Hlavní nádraží Ⓦ praguecityhostel.cz. Clean, modern hostel just a short walk from the main train station, Praha hlavní nádraží. There are three- to twelve-bed mixed dorms, plus double rooms with or without en-suite and kitchen facilities. Also, a communal kitchen and free internet, but breakfast isn't included. Kč

ACCOMMODATION

IMPERIAL MAP PAGE 82, POCKET MAP J11. **Na poříčí 15** Ⓜ **Náměstí Republiky** Ⓦ **hotel-imperial.cz.** Despite describing itself as Art Deco, this place is actually more of an Art Nouveau masterpiece. Built in 1914, the public rooms are simply dripping with period ceramic friezes; the rest of the hotel is standard twenty-first-century luxury. KčKčKčKč

NYX HOTEL MAP PAGE 82, POCKET MAP H13. **Panská 9** Ⓜ **Můstek** Ⓦ **nyx-hotels. com/prague.** One of the capital's most striking but affordable hotels, just a schnitzel's throw from Wenceslas Square. The bold interiors and ahead-of-the-curve artwork choices create a memorable, design-led hotel experience. KčKč

PALACE MAP PAGE 82, POCKET MAP H13. **Panská 12** Ⓜ **Můstek** Ⓦ **palacehotel. cz.** This luxury five-star hotel, just off Wenceslas Square, is renowned for its excellent service and facilities. All the rooms are kept spotless, and the buffet breakfast is top-class. KčKčKč

PAŘÍŽ MAP PAGE 82, POCKET MAP H11. **U Obecního domu 1** Ⓜ **Náměstí Republiky** Ⓦ **hotel-paris.cz.** This is a good top-notch hotel with plenty of fin-de-siècle atmosphere still intact – it was used as the setting for Bohumil Hrabal's *I Served the King of England.* KčKčKč

SALVATOR MAP PAGE 82, POCKET MAP J11. **Truhlářská 10** Ⓜ **Náměstí Republiky** Ⓦ **salvator.cz.** The *Salvator* boasts an extremely good location for the price, just a minutes' walk from náměstí Republiky. The small but clean guest rooms – the cheaper of which have shared facilities – are arranged around a courtyard. The buffet breakfast is delicious, and the staff are friendly and helpful. Kč

Národní třída and southern Nové Město

DANCING HOUSE HOTEL MAP PAGE 91, POCKET MAP F15. **Jiráskovo náměstí 6** Ⓜ **Karlovo náměstí** Ⓦ **dancinghousehotel. com.** Love or hate the *Dancing House*, few can fail to be impressed by how former Czech footballer Vladimír Šmicer has transformed the building into one of Prague's more interesting twenty-first-century hotels. The Fred Royal and Ginger Royal suites tucked within the building's towers, with truly awesome views of Prague Castle, are two of the most desirable rooms in the capital. KčKčKč

HOTEL 16 MAP PAGE 91, POCKET MAP E7. **Kateřinská 16** Ⓜ **Karlovo náměstí** Ⓦ **hotel16.cz.** Friendly family-run hotel offering small, plain but clean en-suite rooms. There's a little terraced garden at the back where you can relax, as well as botanic gardens nearby. KčKč

HOTEL JUNGMANN MAP PAGE 91, POCKET MAP G13. **Jungmannovo náměstí 2** Ⓜ **Můstek** Ⓦ **hotel-jungmann.cz.** Dinky hotel squeezed inside a very tall, narrow building – with no loft – just steps away from the bottom of Wenceslas Square. The guest rooms are spacious – especially the suites – and decked out with tasteful modern decor and furnishings. KčKč

MOSAIC HOUSE MAP PAGE 91, POCKET MAP F15. **Odborů 278/4** M Ⓜ **Karlovo náměstí** Ⓦ **mosaichouse.com.** One of the first hotels in the Czech Republic to

Our Picks

Budget choice: *Czech Inn* see page 127
Central location: *Grand Hotel Praha* see page 124
Boutique bolthole: *Orea place Charles Bridge Aparthotel Prague* see page 123
Room with a view: *Dancing House Hotel* see page 126
Tranquil digs: *Dům u velké boty* see page 123
Luxury abode: *Paříž* see page 126
Eco-friendly pad: *Mosaic House* see page 126

use renewable energy, *Mosaic House* is among the most sustainable places to stay in Prague. Solar panels, water-recycling systems and energy-efficient bathrooms tick all the eco-boxes at this effortlessly cool bolthole. Expect super-comfortable rooms, a bar with undulating light features, cosy café, private spa and secret garden. To top it off, the breakfast is fantastic. KčKčKč

MADHOUSE MAP PAGE 91, POCKET MAP G14. **Spálená 39** Ⓜ **Můstek** Ⓦ **themadhouseprague.com.** The name rather gives the game away at this New Town party hostel, with its funky wall-spanning, hand-painted murals, group dinners, colourful TV lounge and well-equipped kitchen. Kč

MÁNES MAP PAGE 91, POCKET MAP F15. **Myslíkova 20** Ⓜ **Karlovo náměstí** ☎ **778 882 765.** Star ratings mean little in the Czech Republic, but the *Mánes*, named after the nineteenth-century artist, deserves every one of its four twinklers. The fifty guest rooms are finished with contemporary panache, the bathrooms are spacious, and the location near Karlovo náměstí puts you near enough to the city's main sights. KčKč

MISS SOPHIE'S MAP PAGE 91, POCKET MAP E7. **Melounová 3** Ⓜ **I.P. Pavlova** Ⓦ **miss-sophies.com.** A central, slick designer hostel offering everything from cheap dorm beds to fully equipped self-catering apartments. Not your typical rough-and-ready backpacker digs The all-you-can-eat breakfast costs extra. KčKč

Vyšehrad, Vinohrady and Žižkov

ANNA MAP PAGE 103, POCKET MAP F7. **Budečská 17** Ⓦ **Náměstí Míru** Ⓦ **hotelanna. cz.** Plain but smartly appointed rooms,

warm and friendly staff and a decent location make this a popular choice in Vinohrady, with trams and the metro both close by. KčKč

BRIX BAR & HOSTEL MAP PAGE 103, POCKET MAP H5. **Roháčova 132/15** Ⓦ **brixhostel.com.** Cheap and quirky hostel attracting an eclectic crowd of travellers, mainly thanks to its bustling bar and live music most nights. Kč

CLOWN AND BARD MAP PAGE 103, POCKET MAP G6. **Bořivojova 102, tram #5, #9, #26 or #29 to Husinecká** Ⓦ **clownandbard.com.** Žižkov hostel that attracts backpackers who like to party. Still, it's clean and undeniably cheap, stages events and has laundry facilities. Breakfast costs extra (vegetarian option available). Kč

CZECH INN MAP PAGE 103, POCKET MAP G8. **Francouzská 76, tram #4 or #22 to Krymská** Ⓦ **czech-inn.com.** Upbeat designer hostel that feels and looks like a hotel, with friendly and helpful staff. The 36-bed cellar dorm is the biggest in the Czech Republic. Kč

EHRLICH MAP PAGE 103, POCKET MAP H5. **Koněvova 79, tram #9, #10, #11 or #16 to Biskupcova** Ⓦ **hotelehrlich.cz.** Few tourists would choose to stay in Žižkov, but perhaps if they saw this spacious, well-maintained hotel situated on the district's main thoroughfare, they might consider it as an option. Some of the rooms have baths and air conditioning, and there's a decent café in the building. Kč

GALILEO MAP PAGE 103, POCKET MAP F7. **Bruselská 3, tram #6 or #11 to Bruselská** Ⓦ **hotelgalileoprague.com.** Chic, modern hotel furnished with style, offering apartments as well as en-suite double rooms. KčKčKč

ESSENTIALS

Prague's metro is a fast and efficent transport

Arrival

Prague is one of Europe's smaller capital cities. The airport lies just over 10km northwest of the city centre, with only a bus link or taxi to get you into town. Both the international train stations and the main bus terminal are linked to the centre by the fast and efficient metro system.

By plane

Prague's **Václav Havel airport** (ⓦprg.aero) is connected to the city by minibus, bus and taxi. **Prague Airport Shuttle** (ⓦpraguetransport.com) will take you into town for 800Kč for up to four passengers.

The cheapest way to get into town is on local **bus #119** (daily 5am–midnight; every 15–20min; journey time 25min), which stops frequently and ends its journey outside Nádraží Veleslavín metro station. You can buy your ticket from the public transport (DP) information desk in arrivals (daily 7am–9pm), or from the nearby machines. If you're going to use public transport while in Prague, you might as well buy a pass straight away (see page 131). If you arrive between midnight and 5am, you can catch the hourly **night bus** #910 to Divoká Šárka, the terminus for night tram #91, which will take you on to Národní in the centre of town. Another cheap alternative is **Linka AE** (Airport Express), which connects to Dejvická metro (60Kč) and the main train station, Praha hlavní nádraží (daily 5.45am–10.05pm; every 30min; 60Kč).

If you're thinking of taking a **taxi** from the airport, make sure you choose the official airport taxi company svez. se airport transport operated by TICK TACK s.r.o. (ⓟ266 778 899, ⓦtaxi-airport-prague.com). You can also book airport transfers through Prague-based travel agency Avantgarde Prague (ⓦavantgarde-prague.com).

By train

International trains arrive either at Praha hlavní nádraží, on the edge of Nové Město and Vinohrady, or at Praha-Holešovice, which lies north of the city centre. At both stations, you'll find exchange outlets, 24hr left-luggage offices (*úschovna zavazadel*) and accommodation agencies (plus a tourist office at Hlavní nádraží). Both stations are located on metro lines, and Hlavní nádraží is only a five-minute walk from Václavské náměstí (Wenceslas Square).

By bus

Prague's **main bus terminal** is Praha-Florenc (ⓦFlorenc), on the eastern edge of Nové Město, where virtually all long-distance international and domestic services terminate. There's a tourist office here, as well as a left-luggage office and a computer for checking bus times.

Getting around

The centre of Prague is reasonably small and best explored on foot. At some point, however, particularly to reach some of the more widely dispersed attractions, you'll need to use the city's cheap and efficient public transport system (*dopravní podnik* or DP; ⓦdpp.cz), which comprises the metro and a network of trams and buses. You can get free maps, tickets and passes from the DP **information offices** (ⓟ296 191 817) at both airport terminals (daily 7am–9pm), or from Nádraží Veleslavín metro (Mon–Fri 6am–8pm, Sat 9.30am–5pm), Můstek metro (daily 7am–9pm), Anděl metro (daily 7am–9pm), Hradčanská metro (Mon–Fri 6am–8pm, Sat 9.30am–5pm) and the main railway station, Praha hlavní nádraží (Mon–Fri 6am–10pm, Sat & Sun 7am–9pm).

Tickets and passes

Most Praguers buy annual passes, and to avoid having to understand the complexities of the single ticket system, you too are best off buying a **travel pass** (*jízdenka*) for either 24 hours (*1 den*; 120Kč) or three days (*3 dny*; 330Kč); no photos or ID are needed, though you must punch it to validate when you first use it. All the passes are available from DP outlets and ticket machines.

Despite the multitude of buttons on the **ticket machines** – found inside all metro stations and at some bus and tram stops – there are just two basic choices. The 30Kč version (*krátkodobá*) allows you to travel for 30 minutes on the trams or buses, or up to five stops on the metro; it's also known as a *nepřestupní jízdenka*, or "no change ticket", although you can in fact change metro lines (but not buses or trams). The 40Kč version (*základní*) is valid for 90 minutes, during which you may change trams, buses or metro lines as many times as you like, hence its alternative name, *přestupní jízdenka*, or "changing ticket". A full-price ticket is called *plnocenná*; discounted tickets (*zvýhodněna*) are available for children aged 6–15; under-6s travel free.

To buy a ticket from one of the machines, press the appropriate button followed by the *výdej/*enter button, then put your money in. The machines do give change, but another option if you don't have enough coins is to buy your ticket from a tobacconist (*tabák*), street kiosk, newsagent, PIS (Prague Information Service) office or any other place that displays the yellow DP sticker. When you enter the metro, or board a tram or bus, validate your ticket in one of the machines to hand.

There are no barriers, but plain-clothes inspectors (*revizoři*) make random checks and will issue an on-the-spot fine of 800Kč to anyone caught without a valid ticket or pass; controllers should show you their ID (a small metal disc) and give you a receipt (*paragon*).

Metro

Prague's futuristic, Soviet-built **metro** is fast, smooth and ultra-clean, running daily 5am till midnight with trains every two minutes during peak hours, slowing down to every four to ten minutes by late evening. Its three lines intersect at various points in the city centre.

The stations are discreetly marked above ground with the metro logo, in green (line A), yellow (line B) or red (line C). Inside the metro, *výstup* means exit and *přestup* will lead you to one of the connecting lines. The digital clock at the end of the platform tells you what time it is and how long it was since the last train.

Trams

The electric tram (*tramvaj*) system negotiates Prague's hills and cobbles with remarkable dexterity. Modern rolling stock is gradually being introduced, but most of Prague's trams (traditionally red and cream) date back to the Communist era. After the metro, trams are the fastest and most efficient way of getting around, running every six to eight minutes at peak times, and every five to fifteen minutes at other times – check the timetables posted at every stop (*zastávka*), which list the departure times from that stop. Note that it is the custom for younger folk to vacate their seat when an older person enters the carriage.

Tram #22, which runs from Vinohrady to Hradčany via the centre of town and Malá Strana, is a good, cheap way of sightseeing, though you should beware of pickpockets. **Night trams** (*noční tramvaje*; #91–99; every 30–40min; roughly midnight–4.30am) run on different routes from the daytime ones, though at some point all night trams pass along Lazarská in Nové Město.

Buses
You're unlikely to need to get on a **bus** (*autobus*) in Prague, since most of them keep well out of the centre. If you're intent upon visiting the zoo, staying in one of the city's more obscure suburbs, or taking the cheap option to the airport, you will need to use them: their hours of operation are similar to those of the trams (though generally less frequent). **Night buses** (*noční autobusy*) run once an hour midnight–5am.

Ferries and boats
Though few would regard them as a part of the public transport system, a handful of small summer **ferry services** (*přívoz*) operate on the Vltava between the islands and the riverbanks (April–Oct daily 6am–10pm, every 30min). In the summer months there are also regular boat trips on the River Vltava run by the PPS (Pražská paroplavební společnost; Ⓦparoplavba.cz) from just south of Jiráskův, most on Rašínovo nábřeží. Three boats a day in summer run to Troja (see page 117) in the northern suburbs (April & Sept Sat & Sun; May–Aug daily; 160Kč one-way).

The PPS also offers boat trips around Prague (May–Sept daily every 1–2hr; 220–290Kč) on board a 1930s paddle steamer.

Taxis
Taxis are, theoretically at least, relatively cheap. However, many Prague taxi drivers will attempt to overcharge, particularly at taxi ranks close to the tourist sights. Officially, the initial fare on the meter should be around 40Kč plus around 20Kč/km within Prague and 4–6Kč/min waiting time. The best advice is to have your hotel or pension call you one – you then qualify for a cheaper rate – rather than hail one or pick one up at the taxi ranks. The cab company with the best reputation is AAA Taxi (Ⓣ14014, Ⓦaaataxi.cz), which has metered taxis all over Prague.

Directory A–Z

Accessible travel
The *Accessible Prague/Přístupná Praha* guidebook is available from the Prague Wheelchair Association (Pražská organizace vozíčkářů), Benediktská 6 Ⓦpov.cz.

Addresses
The street name is always written before the building number in Prague addresses. The city is divided into numbered postal districts: of the areas covered in the Guide, central Prague is Prague 1; southern Nové Město and half of Vinohrady is Prague 2; the rest of Vinohrady and Žižkov is Prague 3; Holešovice is Prague 7.

Bike rental
City Bike is a reliable rental centre, at Královdorská 5. April–Oct daily 9am–7pm; Ⓣ776 180 284, Ⓦcitybike-prague.com; ⓂNáměstí Republiky.

Children
While it's not particularly ideal for children and babies – lots of walking plus cobblestones can make it

particularly hard on prams as well as little legs – Prague still has plenty to offer. There are plenty of parks and gardens to explore and they can provide a bit of respite from the busy centre. There's also the castle (straight out of a fairy-tale), the zoo, the Petřín funicular and a ride on the tram or a boat if you're stuck for ideas.

Cinema

Cinema tickets still cost less than 250Kč. Most films are shown in the original language with subtitles (*titulky* or *české titulky*); some blockbusters are dubbed (*dabing* or *česká verze*). Occasionally, you can get to see a Czech film with English subtitles (*anglický titulky*).

Crime

There are two main types of police: the **Policie** are the national force, with white shirts, navy blue jackets and grey trousers, while the **Městská** policie, run by the Prague city authorities, are distinguishable by their all-black uniforms. The main central police station is at Bartolomějská 6, Staré Město.

Cultural institutes

American Center, Tržiště13 ⓦ americkecentrum.cz; **Austrian Cultural Institute**, Jungmannovo náměstí 18 ⓦ oekfprag.at; **Instituto Cervantes**, Na rybníčku 6 ⓦ praga. cervantes.es; **Goethe Institut**, Masarykovo nábřeží 32 ⓦ goethe.de/ prag; **Institut Français**, Štěpánská 35 ⓦ ifp.cz; **Instituto Italiano di Cultura**, Šporkova 14 ⓦ iicpraga.esteri.it.

Electricity

The standard continental 220 volts AC. Most European appliances should work as long as you have an adaptor for continental-style two-pin round plugs. North Americans will need this plus a transformer.

Embassies

Australia, Klimentská 10, Nové Město (☎ 221 729 260; ⓜ Náměstí Republiky); **Canada**, Ve Struhách 2, Dejvic (☎ 272 101 800, ⓦ canada.cz; ⓜ Hradčanská); **Ireland**, Tržiště 13, Malá Strana (☎ 257 011 280, ⓦ embassyofireland. cz; ⓜ Malostranská); **New Zealand**, Václavské náměstí 11, Nové Město (☎ 234 784 777; ⓜ Můstek); **South Africa**, Ruská 65, Vršovice (☎ 267 311 114, ⓦ saprague.cz; ⓜ Flora); **UK**, Thunovská 14, Malá Strana (☎ 257 402 111, ⓦ gov.uk/government/world/ organisations/british-embassy-prague; ⓜ Malostranská); **US**, Tržiště 15, Malá Strana (☎ 257 022 000, ⓦ usembassy. cz; ⓜ Malostranská).

Emergencies

All services ☎ 112; Ambulance ☎ 155; Police ☎ 158; Fire ☎ 150.

Health

If you need an English-speaking doctor, head to Nemocnice na Homolce, Roentgenova 2, Motol (☎ 257 271 111). If it's an emergency, dial ☎ 155 for an ambulance. For an emergency dentist, head for Spálená 12, Nové Město (☎ 222 924 268, ⓜ Národní třída). For a 24hr chemist, try Palackého 5 (☎ 224 946 962) or Belgická 37 (☎ 222 513 396).

Internet

The vast majority of hotels and cafés has free wi-fi, and there's free access at the airport and the coach station.

Left luggage

Prague's main bus and train stations each have lockers and/or a 24hr left-luggage office, with instructions in English.

LGBTQ+ Prague

There's a friendly and well-established gay and lesbian scene, with its spiritual heart in the leafy suburbs of Vinohrady and the more run-down neighbourhood of Žižkov. Up-to-date listings are available from ⓦ prague.gayguide.net.

Lost property

The main train stations have lost property offices – look for the sign *ztráty a nálezy* – and there's a central municipal one at Karoliny Světlé 5 (Mon & Wed 8am–5.30pm, Tues & Thurs 8am–4pm, Fri 8am–2pm; ☎ 224 235 085). If you've lost your passport, then get in touch with your embassy (see page 133).

Money

The currency is the Czech crown or *koruna česká* (abbreviated to Kč or CZK). At the time of going to press there were roughly 26Kč to the pound sterling, 23Kč to the euro and around 22Kč to the US dollar. For up-to-date exchange rates, consult ⓦ oanda.com or ⓦ xe.com. Notes come in 100Kč, 200Kč, 500Kč, 1000Kč and 2000Kč (and less frequently 5000Kč) denominations; coins as 1Kč, 2Kč, 5Kč, 10Kč, 20Kč and 50Kč. Banking hours are Monday–Friday 8am–5pm, often with a break at lunchtime. ATMs can be found across the city.

Newspapers

You can get most foreign dailies and magazines at the kiosks located at the bottom of Wenceslas Square, outside metro Můstek.

Opening hours

Shops in Prague are generally open Monday–Friday 9am–5pm, though most tourist shops stay open until 6pm or later. Some shops close by noon or 1pm on Saturday and close all day Sunday, but there's no law against opening on Sundays and many shops in the centre do (including both main supermarkets/department stores). Museums and galleries are generally open Tuesday–Sunday 10am–6pm.

Phones

Most public phones take only phone cards (*telefonní karty*), available from post offices, tobacconists and some shops (prices vary). The best-value ones are prepaid phone cards that give you a phone number and a code to enter. There are instructions in English, and if you press the appropriate button the language on the digital readout will change to English. If you have any problems, ring ☎ 1181 to get through to international information. Phone numbers in Prague consist of nine digits. There are no separate city/area codes in the Czech Republic. Mobile phones from the EU can now be used in the Czech Republic as at home with no roaming charges.

Post

The main 24hr post office (*pošta*) is at Jindřišská 14, Nové Město ☎ 840 111 244; take a ticket and wait for your number to come up. A more tourist-

Eating out price codes

All the cafés and restaurants detailed in this Guide have been graded according to the four price categories listed below. These represent how much you can expect to pay in each establishment for a two-course meal for one, including a drink.

Kč	Kč480–600 (€20–€25)
KčKč	Kč620–840 (€26–€35)
KčKčKč	Kč860–1100 (€36–€45)
KčKčKčKč	Kč1100+ (€46+)

friendly branch exists in the third courtyard of Prague Castle.

Prague CoolPass

The Prague CoolPass (ⓦ praguecoolpass.com) is valid for up to ten days and gives free entry into over seventy sights (though not including the sights of the former Ghetto of Josefov). All in all, the card will save you a lot of hassle, but not necessarily all that much money. The card is available to buy from all travel information and Prague City Tourism offices.

Smoking and vaping

In 2017 the Czech Republic finally introduced a complete smoking ban in public places. At cafés and restaurants, you can no longer light up indoors, but this has simply moved smokers out onto terraces and street seating. Similarly, vaping is also banned indoors.

Time

The Czech Republic is on Central European Time (CET), one hour ahead of Britain and six hours ahead of EST, with the clocks going forward in spring and back again some time in autumn – the exact date changes from year to year. Generally speaking, Czechs use the 24-hour clock.

Tipping

Tipping is normal practice in cafés, bars, restaurants and taxis, usually done simply by rounding up the total. For example, if the waiter tots up the bill and asks you for 138Kč, you should give them 150Kč and tell him to keep the change. Automatic service charges that appear on the bill are not standard Czech practice.

Toilets

Apart from the automatic ones in central Prague, public toilets (*záchody*, *toalety* or WC) are few and far between. In some, you have to buy toilet paper (by the sheet) from the attendant, whom you will also have to pay as you enter. Standards of hygiene can be low. Gentlemen should head for *muži* or *páni*; ladies should head for *ženy* or *dámy*.

Tours

Guided tours are offered all over Prague but the very best can be booked with the local Prague-based agency Avantgarde Prague (ⓦ avantgarde-prague.com). You can sign up for private registered guided tours of the Old Town, Prague Castle and the Jewish Quarter. Avantgarde Prague also organizes a number of activities too, from Czech wine tasting to river cruises.

Tourist information

The tourist office is **Prague City Tourism**, whose main branch is within the **Staroměstská radnice** on Staroměstské náměstí (daily 9am–7pm; ⓦ praguecitytourism.cz). There are additional offices at **Rytířská 12** (daily 9am–7pm), **Staré Město** (daily 9am–7pm; Ⓜ Můstek), in **Wenceslas Square** (daily 10am–6pm), plus an office in the **airport** (daily 9am–7pm). The staff speak English, but their helpfulness varies enormously; however, they can usually answer most enquiries, and can organize accommodation, and sell maps, guides and theatre tickets.

The best **website** for finding your way around the capital is ⓦ mapy.cz, which will help you locate any hotel, restaurant, pub, shop or street in Prague. A more general, informative site is Radio Prague's ⓦ radio.cz/english, which includes the latest news. For information on what's happening in Prague as well as other suggestions for things to see and do, check the website ⓦ expats.cz.

Festivals and events

Epiphany (tří králové)

January 6

The letters K + M + B followed by the date of the new year are chalked on doorways across the capital to celebrate the "Day of the Three Kings" when the Magi came to worship Christ.

Masopust or Carnevale

Shrove Tuesday

The approach of Masopust (the Czech version of Mardi Gras) is celebrated locally in the Žižkov district of Prague, where there's a five-day programme of parties, concerts and parades; a more mainstream series of events takes place under the umbrella of Carnevale, in the city centre.

Easter (Velikonoce)

The age-old sexist ritual of whipping girls' calves with braided birch twigs tied together with ribbons (*pomlázky*) is still practised outside of Prague. To prevent such a fate, the girls are supposed to offer the boys a coloured Easter egg and pour a bucket of cold water over them. You'll see *pomlázky* and Easter eggs on sale, but precious little whipping.

Days of European Film (Dny evropského filmu)

April Ⓦ eurofilmfest.cz

This is the nearest Prague comes to hosting a film festival: a fortnight of arty European films shown at various screens across the capital.

"Burning of the Witches" (Pálení čarodějnic)

April 30

Halloween comes early to the Czech Republic when bonfires are lit across the country, and old brooms thrown out and burned, as everyone celebrates the end of the long winter.

Prague International Marathon

Early May Ⓦ runczech.com

Runners from over fifty countries come to race through the city's cobbled streets and over Charles Bridge.

Prague Spring Festival (Pražské jaro)

May 12–June 2 Box office at Obecní dům, Náměstí Republiky 5, Ⓦ festival.cz

By far the biggest annual arts event and the country's most prestigious international music festival. Established in 1946, it traditionally begins on May 12, the anniversary of Smetana's death, with a procession from his grave in Vyšehrad to the Obecní dům where the composer's *Má vlast* (My Country) is performed in the presence of the president, finishing on June 2 with a rendition of Beethoven's *Ninth Symphony*. Tickets for the festival sell out fast – they are typically made available online in December.

World Roma Festival (Khamoro)

Late May Ⓦ khamoro.cz

International Roma festival of music, dance and film, plus seminars and workshops.

Prague Fringe Festival

Late May/early June Ⓦ praguefringe.com

Your best chance to see English-language theatre in Prague, and good stuff at that. Organizers pack in the shows, and venues are all conveniently located in Malá Strana.

Dance Prague (Tanec Praha)

Four weeks in late May to late June

Ⓦ tanecpraha.cz

An established highlight of Prague's cultural calendar, this international

Public holidays

January 1 New Year's Day; **Easter Monday**; **May 1** May Day; **May 8** VE Day; **July 5** SS Cyril and Methodius Day; **July 6** Jan Hus Day; **September 28** St Wenceslas Day; **October 28** Foundation of the Republic; **November 17** Battle for Freedom and Democracy Day; **December 24** Christmas Eve; **December 25** Christmas Day; **December 26** St Stephen's Day

festival of modern dance takes place at venues throughout the city.

Respect Festival

June Ⓦ rachot.cz/respect-festival
This world music weekend is held at various locations across the city in June, including the Akropolis and Štvanice island.

Burčák

September
For a couple of weeks, stalls on street corners sell the year's partially fermented new wine, known as *burčák*, a misty, heady brew.

Strings of Autumn

Late September to early November
Ⓦ strunypodzimu.cz
Excellent line-up of local and international orchestras and musicians from a wide range of genres. Tickets for this creative festival held in interesting venues go fast.

Christmas markets

December
Markets selling gifts, food and mulled wine (*svářák*) are set up at several places around the city in December: the biggest ones are in Wenceslas Square and the Old Town Square. Temporary ice rinks are also constructed at various locations.

Eve of St Nicholas

December 5
On the evening of December 5, numerous trios, dressed up as St Nicholas (svatý Mikuláš), an angel and a devil, tour the streets. The angel hands out sweets and fruit to children who've been good, while the devil dishes out coal and potatoes to those who've been naughty. The Czech St Nick has white hair and beard, and dresses not in red but in a white priest's outfit, with a bishop's mitre.

Christmas Eve (Štědrý večer)

December 24
Traditionally a day of fasting, broken only when the evening star appears, signalling the beginning of the Christmas feast of carp, potato salad, schnitzel and sweetbreads. Only after the meal are the children allowed to open their presents, which miraculously appear beneath the tree, thanks not to Santa Claus, but to baby Jesus (Ježíšek).

Chronology

895 First recorded Přemyslid duke and first Christian ruler of Prague, Bořivoj, baptized by saints Cyril and Methodius.

929 Prince Václav ("Good King Wenceslas") is martyred by his pagan brother Boleslav the Cruel.

973 Under Boleslav the Pious, Prague becomes a bishopric.

1212 Otakar I secures a royal title for himself and his descendants, who thereafter become kings of Bohemia.

1305 Václav II dies heirless, ending the Přemyslid dynasty.

1346–78 During the reign of Holy Roman Emperor Charles IV, Prague enjoys its first Golden Age as the city is transformed by building projects into a fitting imperial capital.

1389 Three thousand Jews slaughtered in the worst pogrom of the medieval period.

1415 Czech religious reformer Jan Hus is found guilty of heresy and burnt at the stake in Konstanz (Constance).

1419 Prague's first defenestration. Hus's followers, known as the Hussites, throw several councillors to their deaths from the windows of Prague's Nové Město's town hall.

1420 Battle of Vítkov (a hill in Prague). Jan Žižka leads the Hussites to victory over papal forces.

1434 Battle of Lipany. The radical Hussites are defeated by an army of moderates and Catholics.

1526 Habsburg rule in Prague begins, as Emperor Ferdinand I is elected King of Bohemia.

1576–1611 Emperor Rudolf II establishes Prague as the royal seat of power, and ushers in the city's second Golden Age, summoning artists, astronomers and alchemists from all of Europe.

1618 Prague's second defenestration. Two Catholic governors are thrown from the windows of Prague Castle by Bohemian Protestants. The Thirty Years' War begins.

1620 Battle of the White Mountain, just outside Prague. The Protestants, under the "Winter King" Frederick of the Palatinate, are defeated by the Catholic forces; 27 Protestant nobles are executed on the Old Town Square.

1648 The (Protestant) Swedes are defeated on Charles Bridge by Prague's Jewish and student populations. The Thirty Years' War ends.

1713 Plague kills 13,000.

1757 During the Seven Years' War, Prague is besieged and bombarded by the Prussians.

1781 Edict of Tolerance issued by Emperor Joseph II, allowing a large degree of freedom of worship for the first time in 150 years.

1848 Uprising in Prague eventually put down by Habsburg commander Alfred Prince Windischgätz. The ensuing reforms allow Jews to settle outside the ghetto for the first time.

1918 The Habsburg Empire collapses due to defeat in World War I. Czechoslovakia founded.

1920 Tomáš Masaryk elected as first president of Czechoslovakia.

1935 Edvard Beneš elected as the second president of Czechoslovakia.

1938 According to the Munich Agreement drawn up by Britain, France, Fascist Italy and Nazi Germany, the Czechs are forced to secede the border regions of the Sudetenland to Hitler.

1939 In March, the Germans invade and occupy the rest of the Czech Lands. Slovakia declares independence.

1941 Prague's Jews deported to Terezín (Theresienstadt) before being sent to the concentration camps.

1942 Nazi leader Reinhard Heydrich assassinated in Prague. The two villages of Lidice and Ležáky are annihilated in retaliation.

1945 On May 5, the Prague Uprising against the Nazis begins. On May 9, the Russians liberate the city. The city's ethnic German population is brutally expelled.

1946 Communist Party wins up to forty percent of the vote in the first postwar general election. Beneš formally re-elected as president.

1948 The Communist Party seizes power in a bloodless coup in February. Thousands flee the country. Jan Masaryk, Foreign Minister and son of the former president, dies in mysterious circumstances. Beneš resigns as president, replaced by Communist leader, Klement Gottwald.

1952 Twelve leading Party members (eleven of them Jewish) sentenced to death as traitors in Prague's infamous show trials.

1953 Klement Gottwald dies five days after Stalin.

1968 During the "Prague Spring", reformers within the Party abolish censorship. Soviet troops invade and stop the reform movement. Thousands go into exile.

1977 243 Czechs and Slovaks, including playwright Václav Havel, sign the Charter 77 manifesto, reigniting the dissident movement.

1989 After two weeks of popular protest, known as the Velvet Revolution, the Communist government resigns. Havel is elected as president.

1993 Czechoslovakia splits into the Czech Republic and Slovakia. Havel is elected as Czech president.

1999 The Czech Republic joins NATO.

2002 In August, Prague is devastated by the worst floods in 200 years.

2003 Václav Klaus, former Finance Minister and Prime Minister, is elected as the second Czech president.

2004 The Czech Republic enters the European Union (EU), together with nine other accession countries, including Slovakia.

2011 Václav Havel dies, at the age of 75.

2013 Czechs elect Miloš Zeman into office in the country's first direct presidential election.

2017/18 The Czechs hold key elections which dictate the future direction the country will take.

2018 Miloš Zeman narrowly defeats Jiří Drahoš and is elected for second term in office.

2023 Petr Pavel is elected as president in a landslide win.

Czech

A modicum of English is spoken in Prague's central restaurants and hotels, and among the city's younger generation. Any attempt to speak

Czech will be heartily appreciated, though don't be discouraged if people seem not to understand, as most will be unaccustomed to hearing foreigners stumble through their language. Unfortunately, Czech (**český**) is a highly complex western Slav tongue, into which you're unlikely to make much headway during a short stay.

Pronunciation

English-speakers often find Czech impossibly difficult to pronounce: just try the Czech tongue-twister, *strč prst skrz krk* (stick your finger down your neck). The good news is that, apart from a few special letters, each letter and syllable is pronounced as it's written – the trick is to always stress the first syllable of a word, no matter what its length; otherwise, you'll render it unintelligible.

Short and long vowels

Czech has both short and long vowels (the latter being denoted by a variety of accents):

a like the u in c**u**p
á as in f**a**ther
e as in p**e**t
é as in f**ai**r
ě like the ye in **ye**s
i or y as in p**i**t
í or ý as in s**ea**t
o as in n**o**t
ó as in d**oo**r
u like the oo in b**oo**k
ů or ú like the oo in f**oo**l

Vowel combinations and diphthongs

There are very few diphthongs in Czech, so any combinations of vowels other than those below should be pronounced as two separate syllables.
au like the ou in f**ou**l
ou like the oe in f**oe**

Consonants and accents

There are no silent consonants, but it's worth remembering that r and l can form a half-syllable if standing between two other consonants or at the end of a word, as in Brno (Br-no)

or Vltava (Vl-ta-va). The consonants listed below are those which differ substantially from the English. Accents look daunting, particularly the háček, which appears above c, d, n, r, s, t and z, but the only one which causes a lot of problems is ř, probably the most difficult letter to say in the entire language – even Czech toddlers have to be taught how to say it.

c like the **ts** in boats
č like the **ch** in chicken
ch like the **ch** in the Scottish loch
ď like the **d** in duped
g always as in goat, never as in general
h always as in have, but more energetic
j like the **y** in yoke
kd pronounced as **gd**
mě pronounced as **mnye**
ň like the **n** in nuance
p softer than the English **p**
r as in rip, but often rolled
ř approximately like the sound of **r** and **ž** combined
š like the **sh** in shop
ť like the **t** in tutor
ž like the **s** in pleasure; but at the end of a word like the **sh** in shop

Words and phrases

Basics

Yes ano
No ne
Please/excuse me prosím vás
Don't mention it není zač
Sorry pardon
Thank you děkuju
Bon appétit dobrou chuť
Bon voyage šťastnou cestu
Hello/goodbye (informal) ahoj
Hello (formal) dobrý den
Goodbye (formal) na shledanou
Good morning dobré ráno
Good evening dobrý večer
Good night (when leaving) dobrou noc
How are you? jak se máte?
I'm English ja jsem angličan(ka)
    /Irish /ir(ka)

/**Scottish** /skot(ka)
/**Welsh** /velšan(ka)
/**American** /američan(ka)
Do you speak English? mluvíte anglicky?
I don't speak Czech nemluvím česky
I don't speak German nemluvím německy
I don't understand nerozumím
I understand rozumím
I don't know nevím
Speak slowly mluvte pomalu
How do you say that in Czech? jak se to
řekne česky?
Could you write it down for me? mužete
mi to napsat?
Today dnes
Yesterday včera
Tomorrow zítra
The day after tomorrow pozítří
Now hned
Later později
Wait a minute! moment!
Leave me alone! dej mi pokoj!
Go away! jdi pryč!
Help! pomoc!
This one toto
A little trochu
Another one ještě jedno
Large/small velký/malý
More/less více/méně
Good/bad dobrý/špatný
Cheap/expensive levný/drahý
Hot/cold horký/studený
With/without s/bez
The bill please zaplatím prosím
Do you have ...? máte ...?
We don't have nemáme
We do have máme

Questions

What? co?
Where? kde?
When? kdy?
Why? proč?
Which one? který/která/které?
This one? tento/tato/toto?
How many? kolik?
What time does it open? kdy máte
otevřeno?
What time does it close? kdy zavíráte?

Getting around

Over here tady
Over there tam
Left nalevo
Right napravo
Straight on rovně
Where is ...? kde je ...?
How do I get to Prague? jak se dostanu
do Prahy?
How do I get to the...? jak se dostanu k...?
By bus autobusem
By train vlakem
By car autem
On foot pěšky
By taxi taxíkem
Stop here, please zastavte tady, prosím
Ticket jízdenka/lístek
Return ticket zpateční
Train station nádraží
Bus station autobusové nádraží
Bus stop autobusová zastávka
When's the next train to Prague? kdy jede
další vlak do Prahy?
Is it going to Prague? jede to do Prahy?
Do I have to change? musím přestupovat?
Do I need a reservation? musím mít
místenku?
Is this seat free? je tu volno?
May we (sit down)? můžeme (se sednout)?

Accommodation

Are there any rooms available? máte volné
pokoje?
Do you have a double room? máte jeden
dvoulůžkový pokoj?
For one night na jednu noc
With shower se sprchou
With bath s koupelnou
How much is it? kolík to stojí?
With breakfast? se snídaní?

Some signs

Entrance vchod
Exit východ
Toilets záchody/toalety
Men muži
Women ženy
Ladies dámy
Gentlemen pánové
Open otevřeno

Closed zavřeno
Pull/Push sem/tam
Danger! pozor!
Hospital nemocnice
No smoking kouření zakázáno
No entry vstup zakázán
Arrival příjezd
Departure odjezd

Days of the week

Monday pondělí
Tuesday uterý
Wednesday středa
Thursday čtvrtek
Friday pátek
Saturday sobota
Sunday neděle
Day den
Week týden
Month měsíc
Year rok

Months of the year

Many Slav languages have their own
highly individual systems in which the
words for the names of the months
are descriptive nouns, sometimes
beautifully apt for the month in
question.
January leden (ice)
February únor (hibernation)
March březen (birch)
April duben (oak)
May květen (blossom)
June červen (red)
July červenec (red)
August srpen (sickle)
September zaří (blazing)
October říjen (rutting)
November listopad (leaves falling)
December prosinec (millet porridge)

Numbers

1 jeden
2 dva
3 tři
4 čtyři
5 pět
6 šest
7 sedm
8 osm
9 devět
10 deset
11 jedenáct
12 dvanáct
13 třináct
14 čtrnáct
15 patnáct
16 šestnáct
17 sedmnáct
18 osmnáct
19 devatenáct
20 dvacet
21 dvacetjedna
30 třicet
40 čtyřicet
50 padesát
60 šedesát
70 sedmdesát
80 osmdesát
90 devadesát
100 sto
101 sto jedna
155 sto padesát pět
200 dvě stě
300 tři sta
400 čtyři sta
500 pět set
600 šest set
700 sedm set
800 osm set
900 devět set
1000 tisíc

Food and drink terms

Basics

chléb bread
chlebíček (open) sandwich
cukr sugar
hořčice mustard
houska round roll
knedlíky dumplings
křen horseradish
lžíce spoon
maso meat
máslo butter
med honey
mléko milk
moučník dessert

nápoje drinks
na zdraví! cheers!
nůž knife
oběd lunch
obloha garnish
ocet vinegar
ovoce fruit
pečivo rolls
pepř pepper
polévka soup
předkrmy starters
přílohy side dishes
rohlík finger roll
ryby fish
rýže rice
sklenice glass
snídaně breakfast
sůl salt
šálek cup
talíř plate
tartarská omáčka tartare sauce
večeře supper/dinner
vejce eggs
vidlička fork
volské oko fried egg
zeleniny vegetables

Common terms

čerstvý fresh
domácí home-made
dušený stew/casserole
grilovaný roast on the spit
kyselý sour
na kmíně with caraway seeds
na roštu grilled
nadívaný stuffed
nakládaný pickled
(za)pečený baked/roast
plněný stuffed
s máslem with butter
sladký sweet
slaný salted
smažený fried in breadcrumbs
studený cold
syrový raw
sýrový with cheese
teplý hot
uzený smoked
vařený boiled

Soups

boršč beetroot soup
bramborová potato soup
čočková lentil soup
fazolová bean soup
hovězí vývar beef broth
hrachová pea soup
kuřecí thin chicken soup
rajská tomato soup
zeleninová vegetable soup

Fish

kapr carp
losos salmon
makrela mackerel
platys flounder
pstruh trout
rybí filé fillet of fish
sardinka sardine
štika pike
treska cod
zavináč herring/rollmop

Meat dishes

bažant pheasant
biftek beef steak
čevapčiči spicy meatballs
dršťky tripe
drůbež poultry
guláš goulash
hovězí beef
husa goose
játra liver
jazyk tongue
kachna duck
klobásy sausages
kotleta cutlet
kuře chicken
kýta leg
ledvinky kidneys
řízek steak
roštěná sirloin
salám salami
sekaná meat loaf
skopové maso mutton
slanina bacon
svíčková fillet of beef
šunka ham
telecí veal
vepřový pork

CZECH

vepřový řízek breaded pork
cutlet or schnitzel
zajíc hare
žebírko ribs

Vegetables

brambory potatoes
brokolice broccoli
celer celery
cibule onion
červená řepa beetroot
česnek garlic
chřest asparagus
čočka lentils
fazole beans
houby mushrooms
hranolky chips, French fries
hrášek peas
květák cauliflower
kyselá okurka pickled gherkin
kyselé zelí sauerkraut
lečo ratatouille
lilek aubergine
mrkev carrot
okurka cucumber
pórek leek
rajče tomato
ředkev radish
špenát spinach
zelí cabbage
žampiony mushrooms

Fruit, cheese and nuts

arašídy peanuts
banán banana
borůvky blueberries
broskev peach
brusinky cranberries
bryndza goat's cheese in brine
citrón lemon

grep grapefruit
hermelín Czech brie
hrozny grapes
hruška pear
jablko apple
jahody strawberries
kompot stewed fruit
maliny raspberries
mandle almonds
meruňka apricot
niva semi-soft, crumbly, blue cheese
ostružiny blackberries
oštěpek heavily smoked, curd cheese
pivní sýr cheese flavoured with beer
pomeranč orange
rozinky raisins
švestky plums
třešně cherries
tvaroh fresh curd cheese
uzený sýr smoked cheese
vlašské ořechy walnuts

Drinks

čaj tea
destiláty spirits
káva coffee
koňak brandy
láhev bottle
minerální (voda) mineral (water)
mléko milk
pivo beer
presso espresso
s ledem with ice
soda soda
suché víno dry wine
šumivý fizzy
svařené víno/svařak mulled wine
tonic tonic
vinný střik white wine with soda
víno wine

The alphabet

In the Czech alphabet, letters which feature a **háček** (as in the č of the word itself) are considered separate letters and appear in Czech indexes immediately after their more familiar cousins. More confusingly, the consonant combination ch is also considered as a separate letter and appears in Czech indexes after the letter h.

A glossary of Czech terms

brána gate
český Bohemian
chrám cathedral
divadlo theatre
dům house
hora mountain
hospoda/hostinec pub
hrad castle
hřbitov cemetery
kaple chapel
katedrála cathedral
kavárna coffee house
klášter monastery/convent
kostel church
koupaliště swimming pool
Labe River Elbe
lanovka funicular/cable car
les forest
město town
most bridge
muzeum museum
nábřeží embankment

nádraží train station
náměstí square
ostrov island
palác palace
památník memorial or monument
pasáž interior shopping arcade
pivnice pub
radnice town hall
restaurace restaurant
sad park
sál room/hall
schody steps
svatý/svatá saint; often abbreviated to sv
třída avenue
ulice street
věž tower
vinárna wine bar/cellar
Vltava River Moldau
vrchy hills
výstava exhibition
zahrada garden
zámek chateau

SMALL PRINT

Publishing Information
Fifth edition 2023

Distribution
UK, Ireland and Europe
Apa Publications (UK) Ltd; sales@roughguides.com
United States and Canada
Ingram Publisher Services; ips@ingramcontent.com
Australia and New Zealand
Booktopia; retailer@booktopia.com.au
Worldwide
Apa Publications (UK) Ltd; sales@roughguides.com
Special Sales, Content Licensing and CoPublishing
Rough Guides can be purchased in bulk quantities at discounted prices. We can create special editions, personalised jackets and corporate imprints tailored to your needs. sales@roughguides.com.
roughguides.com
Printed in Turkey
This book was produced using **Typefi** automated publishing software.

A catalogue record for this book is available from the British Library
The publishers and authors have done their best to ensure the accuracy and currency of all the information in **Pocket Rough Guide Prague**, however, they can accept no responsibility for any loss, injury, or inconvenience sustained by any traveller as a result of information or advice contained in the guide.

Rough Guide Credits

Editor: Joanna Reeves
Cartography: Katie Bennett
Picture editor: Piotr Kala
Layout: Pradeep Thapliyal
Original design: Richard Czapnik
Head of DTP and Pre-Press: Rebeka Davies
Head of Publishing: Sarah Clark

About the author
Beth Williams is a travel writer and editor for Rough Guides. She has lived in the USA and Germany, before coming home to East London. Her adventures have taken her to Southeast Asia, the States and through much of continental Europe. She likes seeking out new dishes that she hasn't tried before and is a firm believer that you can tell a lot about a country from its local food market.

Help us update

We've gone to a lot of effort to ensure that this edition of the **Pocket Rough Guide Prague** is accurate and up-to-date. However, things change – places get "discovered", opening hours are notoriously fickle, restaurants and rooms raise prices or lower standards. If you feel we've got it wrong or left something out, we'd like to know, and if you can remember the address, the price, the hours, the phone number, so much the better.

Please send your comments with the subject line "**Pocket Rough Guide Prague Update**" to mail@uk.roughguides.com. We'll credit all contributions and send a copy of the next edition (or any other Rough Guide if you prefer) for the very best emails.

Photo Credits

(Key: T-top; C-centre; B-bottom; L-left; R-right)

Blatouch 110
Jan Flake Fridrich/La Veranda 79
Pylones 97
Restaurant Pod Věží 52
Savoy cafe 51
Shutterstock 1, 2T, 2BL, 2C, 2BR, 4, 5, 6, 10, 11T, 11B, 12BL, 12/13B, 12/13T, 13C, 14B, 14T, 15B, 15T, 16B, 16T, 17B, 17T, 18T, 18C, 18B, 19T, 19C, 19B, 20T, 20C, 20B, 21T, 21C, 21B, 22T, 22C, 22B, 23T, 23C, 23B, 24/25, 26, 29, 30, 31, 32, 33, 35, 36, 37, 38, 39, 40, 41, 44, 45, 46, 47, 48, 49, 50, 53, 54, 55, 58, 59, 60, 61, 62, 63, 64, 65, 66, 67, 68, 69, 70, 71, 73, 74, 75, 76, 77, 78, 80, 81, 83, 84, 85, 86, 87, 88, 89, 90, 92, 93, 94, 95, 96, 98, 99, 100, 101, 102, 104, 105, 106, 107, 108, 109, 111, 112, 114, 115, 116, 117, 118, 119, 120/121, 128/129

Cover: The Astronomical Clock **Sergii Figurnyi/Shutterstock**

Index

NOTES